Discovering Sharks

UNDERWATER NATURALIST
Bulletin of the American Littoral Society
Special Double Issue
Volume 19, Number 4 and Volume 20, Number 1

Sometimes a topic presents itself that is so important and so big that it can't be presented properly within the pages of a standard length UNDERWATER NATURALIST. Such is the case with sharks. The editors felt that Littoral Society members would be fascinated to learn about these often maligned and magnificent creatures. The result is this special double issue. (Additional copies are available for $10.00.)

EDITORIAL STAFF:

D.W. Bennett, *Editor*

A.L. Pacheco, *Articles*   Hannah Johnson, *Copy*
Michele Cox, *Production*   Elizabeth Cousins, *Circulation*

Samuel H. Gruber, *Special Issue Editor*

Special Issue Editorial Board:
Jeffrey C. Carrier   Robert E. Hueter   Sanford Moss

UNDERWATER NATURALIST is the bulletin of the American Littoral Society, Highlands, NJ 07732, and is mailed to members as a part of their annual dues: $15 for students/seniors; $25 for individuals and families; $30 for clubs and libraries (USA), and $35 for foreign. Printed in the United States of America, American Littoral Society, December 1990. Note: Past volumes of UNDERWATER NATURALIST and individual articles are available on microfiche from UMI, Ann Arbor, MI 48106.

Special Publication No. 14 of the American Littoral Society

Cover Photograph by Doug Perrine
©1990 Inner Space Visions

Copyright©1991 by American Littoral Society, Highlands, NJ 07732
All Rights Reserved
Library of Congress Catalog Card Number: 91-71245
Printed in the United States of America

Discovering Sharks

A volume honoring
the work of Stewart Springer

Edited by
Samuel H. Gruber

AMERICAN LITTORAL SOCIETY
HIGHLANDS, NEW JERSEY 07732

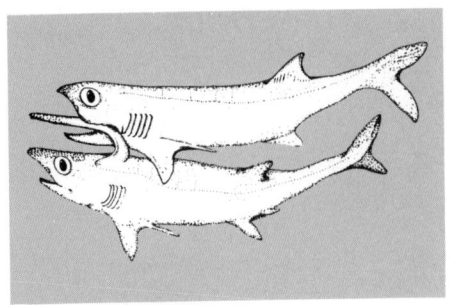

Contents

Foreword
SAMUEL H. GRUBER 1

Preface
PERRY W. GILBERT 3

Life History Notes
on Stewart Springer
GEORGE H. BURGESS 4

Life Style of the Sharks
SAMUEL H. GRUBER 7

The Evolution
and Diversity of Sharks
LEONARD J.V. COMPAGNO 15

Shadows in Time -
A Capsule History of Sharks
RICHARD LUND 23

Shark Early Life History —
One Reason Sharks Are
Vulnerable to Overfishing
STEVE BRANSTETTER 29

Anatomical Features of Sharks
And Their Allies
SANFORD MOSS 35

The Unique Role
of Two Liver Products
In Suiting Sharks
to Their Environment
THOMAS B. THORSON 41

The Sensory World of Sharks
ROBERT E. HUETER
and PERRY W. GILBERT 48

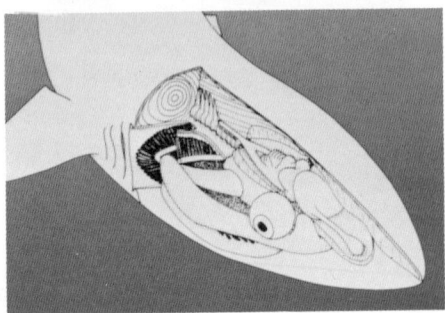

Shark Reproduction:
Parental Investment
and Limited Fisheries —
An Overview
HAROLD L. PRATT, JR..
and JOSÉ I. CASTRO 56

From Egg to Placenta:
Placental Reproduction in Sharks
WILLIAM C. HAMLETT 61

The Reproductive Biology
of Lamnoid Sharks
R. GRANT GILMORE 64

Feeding Biology of Sharks
BRAD WETHERBEE 74

The Ravenous Mako
CHUCK STILLWELL 77

How Deep Do Sharks Go?
Reflections on Deep Sea Sharks
EUGENIE CLARK
and EMORY KRISTOF 79

Home Range
of Juvenile Lemon Sharks
JOHN F. MORRISSEY 85

Long Distance Movements
of Atlantic Sharks
From the NMFS Cooperative
Shark Tagging Program
J.G. CASEY
and N. E. KOHLER 87

The Behavior of Sharks:
What Have We Learned?
ARTHUR A. MYRBERG, JR.
and DONALD R. NELSON 92

Shark Attack
and the International
Shark Attack File
GEORGE H. BURGESS 101

Shark Repellents:
How Effective, How Needed?
DONALD R. NELSON 106

Uncovering the Ages of Sharks
and Its Importance
in Fisheries Management
CHARLES S. PIKE III 111

U.S. Shark Fishery Management
For the Atlantic Ocean
THOMAS B. HOFF
and JOSÉ I. CASTRO 112

The Only Good Shark
Is A Dead Shark?
SAMUEL H. GRUBER
and CHARLES A. MANIRE 115

Growth and Aging:
Life History Studies
of the Nurse Shark
JEFFREY C. CARRIER 68

Instruments of Natural Selection:
How Important Are Sharks?
WESLEY R. STRONG, JR. 70

Foreword

This volume, honoring the long and distinguished career of Stewart Springer, owes its genesis to a series of discussions I had late in 1989 with Dery Bennett, executive director of the American Littoral Society. In response to the crisis triggered by the apparent overexploitation of our shark stocks and the pending Secretarial Shark Management Plan, I enquired if the Society would publish a manuscript that John Morrissey and I wrote in support of the Plan. Our article was accepted (Bull. Am. Lit. Soc. 19(1):3-7) and moreover, Dery suggested that the Society would support an entire volume on shark biology and conservation. This special shark volume, I thought, could provide a way to express my gratitude to and admiration for Stewart Springer, certainly one of the major, if not *the* major influence on my scientific career.

I contacted more than 20 potential contributors and explained Dery's suggestion. The response was universally positive — especially since the volume was to honor Stew. It was really gratifying to see how many of my friends and colleagues felt the same as I about Stew.

In my haste to form a slate of knowledgeable authors, I relied heavily on personal acquaintances and inadvertently left out many who could and would have produced excellent articles. For this oversight I am truly sorry.

Dery Bennett and Hannah Johnson were helpful and supportive throughout, and the authors produced thoughtful, interesting articles — on time. Done entirely without compensation, the authors' works represent their donations of time, effort, and expertise to the Society and in honor of Stewart. I am thus grateful to each and every author. However, I am most grateful to the Scientific Editorial Board composed of Drs. Jeff Carrier, Bob Hueter, and Sandy Moss for critically reviewing and editing all 26 manuscripts and discussing their comments with each author. My sincere thanks for their "thankless" task.

Samuel H. Gruber
Miami, Florida
November 27, 1990

Stewart Springer circa 1960.

Preface

by PERRY W. GILBERT

What a pleasure to write the preface to this volume honoring Stewart Springer, for Stew and I have been close friends for more than 30 years. He has been a delightful companion in the field, and for 13 years he was a wise counsellor and member of our American Institute of Biological Sciences (AIBS) Shark Research Panel. For 11 years he served as a valued colleague at the Mote Marine Laboratory in Sarasota, FL, while in charge of our Placida Station.

Stew and I spent a week together in the mid-fifties on board the National Marine Fisheries Service "Oregon I," out of Pascagoula, MS. On this trip Stew introduced me to the tiny, luminescent, deep water sharks *Etmopterus virens* and *Etmopterus schultzi*. I also recall that Stew set a long line and hooked a very lively oceanic whitetip, *Carcharhinus longimanus*. As he was about to bring the shark into the boat, it snapped the wire leader. Three days later, and several hundred miles away, he hooked the shark again and retrieved it and the broken leader — this shark had followed our boat for all that time.

In Mazatlan, Mexico, in the spring of 1964 Stew, Shelly Applegate, Sus Kato, and I watched shark fishermen haul their catch ashore in the early morning hours and counted 17 species. Stew identified all of them for us. Later, on this same trip, as guests of the Mexican government, we visited the prison colony and shark fishery at Las Tres Marias, one of the most modern prisons in the world. There were no bars and the prisoners, who lived with their wives, became our good friends. I remember one young American prisoner who remarked he had been in several jails in the United States but this one beat them all for he had never had it so good.

The AIBS Shark Research Panel, composed of Leonard Schultz, Sid Galler, John Olive, Dave Baldridge, Al Tester, Stew and myself, met two or three times a year. Our job was to stimulate and coordinate shark research in this country and abroad, and to perform our own research on the biology and behavior of sharks. Usually we met at least once a year in Washington, DC, and once or twice a year in Florida, Louisiana, California, or Hawaii. The results of our deliberations have appeared in various books and professional journals.

The Placida Station was located at Charlotte Harbor, one of the few, relatively uncontaminated, large estuaries east of the Mississippi. The Station was very near the Cape Haze Marine Laboratory which was founded by Dr. Eugenie Clark in 1955 and was the forerunner of the Mote Marine Laboratory (MML). Here Stew hosted visiting investigators and student classes from Cornell, acquainting them with the fauna that he knew so well. For years he had been Collector and Director of the Bass Biological Laboratory in nearby Englewood, Florida. Stew also played a prominent role in MML's Red Tide Program. Each week he obtained water samples from 13 stations in Charlotte Harbor and brought them to our headquarters on Siesta Key in Sarasota where they were analyzed.

We owe Stew Springer so much for he has directly, or indirectly, been teacher, wise counsellor, and good friend to all of us who have contributed to this volume. It is most fitting that the articles which follow pay tribute, in some small way, to this fine scientist and scholar.

Life History Notes on Stewart Springer

by GEORGE H. BURGESS

During this century the field of elasmobranch studies has been blessed by a number of prominent workers — the names Garman, Bigelow, Schroeder, and Gilbert immediately come to mind — but one person stands out above all others when discussions turn to sharks. It is safe to say that there isn't a serious student of sharks who hasn't heard of Stewart Springer. We all have consulted, at one time or another, one or more of Stew's many publications. More importantly, he has served as a living source book of firsthand observations and analysis to three generations of elasmobranch workers. The breadth of Springer's knowledge of sharks — his publications cover the gamut of their biology, including life history, systematics, ecology, and fishery management — has placed him in constant demand as a consultant. Many a research project has included, "Check with Stewart Springer," as part of its initial planning. Additionally, Stew has planted the seed for many others by freely sharing his observations and hypotheses in off-the-cuff discussions with colleagues.

Perhaps the most impressive aspect of Springer's career is the way he gained his knowledge. After graduating from high school in Indianapolis in 1924, where he got his first taste of biology as a zoology assistant, Stew attended Butler College for two years while simultaneously supporting himself as a union musician and

Director of the International Shark Attack File and senior biologist in ichthyology at the Florida Museum of Natural History, University of Florida, Gainesville, Burgess is a past president of the American Elasmobranch Society. His research interests include shark conservation, the systematics of deep-sea dogfish sharks, and life history and ecology of nearshore sharks as well as shark attacks.

serving as the first curator of the Children's Museum of Indianapolis. After spending a year as a chemistry technician at the Indianapolis Activated Sludge Plant, he embarked on a southward migration that eventually landed him in Biloxi, MS, in 1929. Prior to this move Stew's biological passion was terrestrial in nature with summer field trips yielding many interesting specimens and observations. Four of his first five papers, in fact, covered herpetological or mammalian subjects, and included among these was the description of a new lizard, *Cnemidophorus velox*, which, to his current surprise, has stood the test of time as a valid species.

Springer spent seven years in Biloxi working as a commercial biological specimen collector and a commercial fisherman. His "hands on" experiences with sea creatures during this period shifted his interest from terrestrial to marine biology and provided his earliest interactions with elasmobranchs. Elasmobranch studies began in earnest while Stew worked at his next position as manager of the Bass Biological Laboratory in Englewood, FL. From 1936-1940 Springer served as the laboratory's resident guide for visiting researchers while continuing to procure biological specimens and fish commercially for sharks. He learned longline and gillnet technologies in the same manner he had learned shrimping and boatsmanship in Biloxi: by asking a lot of questions (in this case of Shark Industries, which operated out of Salerno, FL) and trial and error. During this period Stew published 10 papers, the first two his final forays into the non-ichthyological arena (least shrew and leopard frog) and the remainder on sharks, skates, and rays. His first elasmobranch paper, *Notes on the Sharks of*

Florida, was named the best paper of 1938 by the Florida Academy of Sciences.

When Jack Bass died, the Bass Laboratory closed, and Springer moved on to Islamorada, in the upper Keys, where he managed Florida Marine Products, a commercial sharkfishing operation. Here he first learned some valuable economic facts of life relating to shark populations and the vitamin A contents of their livers. Sharks were the major source of vitamin A at this time. He began to more fully understand the principles of total, accessory, and principal populations and "bank loafers," a term he coined for the few large and old resident sharks with high vitamin A contents that are easily caught during initial fishing activities. Bank loafers lead inexperienced fishermen into thinking they have found a rich fishing ground; unfortunately for Stew and his parent company, too many of the early catches from this area were these kinds of sharks, and the operation folded after a year due to poor catches.

Springer was offered jobs at the University of Miami and Shark Industries and chose the latter. He worked as assistant manager of the largest commercial sharkfishing operation on the East Coast for a short time before he was called to Washington to work with the government's war-time efforts in formulating a shark repellent. Large numbers of aviators were going down over the ocean and stories of shark attack were rampant among pilots, leading to a considerable loss of morale. To quote Springer, "It was okay to give one's life for your country, but to get eaten for it was another matter." Work on a repellent took Stew to Woods Hole, La Jolla, Biloxi, and the Keys, but a truly effective product was never formulated. Stew takes solace in knowing the developed product, "Shark Chaser," saved at least some lives and that the compound provided a psychological lift to many servicemen.

Springer spent 1945 in St. Petersburg, FL, working on development of a dried mullet product intended for use by the British Army's elite Gurka Unit. A devastating hurricane and the end of the war terminated this project, and Stew moved to south Florida where he resumed commercial sharkfishing out of Card Sound. Once again a hurricane proved his nemesis by sinking his vessel, so he returned to Shark Industries in 1947 as port manager. For the next three years Stew worked not only to maximize total shark catches but also to find sharks with vitamin A-rich livers, by selecting specific fishing sites based on season, depth, and his knowledge of migratory patterns. Working without the benefit of tag data, Springer developed fishing strategies from examination of fishery records and frequent, daily quantitative determinations of vitamin A levels. He also made exploratory shark fishing trips to the Bahamas, the southern Caribbean, and Brazil and continued to publish his observations on sharks.

The development of a cheaper source of vitamin A caused the collapse of the shark fishery in 1950, and Stew was hired as station chief of the U.S. Fish and Wildlife Service's (USFWS) Commercial Fisheries Laboratory in Pascagoula, MS. At first "laboratory" was a totally inappropriate word since Springer was asked to start up a USFWS facility that would interact with the commercial sector. Armed only with "an order pad and a vessel," the *RV Oregon*, Stew directed the formation and early growth of what is now the National Marine Fisheries Service's (NMFS) Southeast Fisheries Center, Pascagoula facility. Perhaps the most important development was the Springer-designed exploratory fishing surveys. These field operations provided badly needed data on Gulf of Mexico stocks, areas of exploitable concentrations, and new resources. Equally important were the large collections of marine organisms Springer ordered saved for use by systematists. In particular, our current knowledge of the Gulf of Mexico ichthyofauna was greatly enhanced by these and subsequent USFWS and

NMFS collections. Results of the *Oregon*'s activities and continuing shark studies were reported in a series of publications during this period.

Stew moved to Washington, D.C. in late 1955 to head up the Exploratory Fishing branch of USFWS. He took night courses at George Washington University and, 39 years after starting his education at Butler College, received his bachelor's degree in 1964 at the age of 58. Soon after Springer transferred to Stanford University where he spent three years working on shark fisheries and systematic research projects. While at Stanford he spent a lot of time advising a young student named Leonard Compagno, who was just starting graduate school with George Myers. Stew returned to Washington in 1968 and, after serving as Deputy Assistant Director for the USFWS for a short period, settled into the Systematics Laboratory at the Smithsonian Institution where he remained until his retirement in 1971. He served as an affiliated researcher at the Mote Marine Laboratory for several years while working at his retirement home in Placida, FL, and published his revision of the catsharks in 1979. In 1980 he moved to Gainesville where he has remained active as a research associate at the Florida Museum of Natural History. Springer was awarded the American Elasmobranch Society's Distinguished Service Award in 1988 in honor of a lifetime of research on sharks.

Our knowledge of sharks has been substantially enhanced by Stewart Springer. We owe a great deal of thanks to the "Grand Old Man of Sharks" for his many contributions and contagious enthusiasm for these fascinating creatures.

Blue shark. Photo by H.W. Pratt.

Life Style of the Sharks

by SAMUEL H. GRUBER

A diver descends into the crystal clear waters off Bimini, Bahamas. The living reef comes into sharp focus revealing colors, movement, and a myriad of creatures. Suddenly the diver is aware of a presence — a large shark glides into the area, serene, graceful, and apparently unconcerned with the alien human. As quickly as it arrived, it disappears into the warm blue haze. This first close encounter with a shark leaves a permanent impression on the diver. The initial, intense pangs of cold fear give way to awe and admiration. The creature's size, form, movement, and easy power set it apart from everything else on the reef. Yet overlying the reality of the great fish is a residue of western mythology at odds with the truth.

Later, the diver excitedly tells and retells the story of this encounter. Then the questions come. What kind of shark was it? Are they common, dangerous? How big do they get? Do they live in schools? How old are they?

These kinds of questions define the life-style of all shark species. The systematic study of these very general questions is subsumed under the Theory of Life History and can teach us much about the ecological role and especially the biological evolution of sharks. In a more practical vein, understanding the life style of sharks can provide important insights into protecting them from over harvesting by fishermen.

Throughout the following pages, I will acquaint you with life history theory, what it can tell us, how it is studied, and especially how the life style of most

Gruber is professor of marine biology and fisheries at the University of Miami's Rosenstiel School of Marine and Atmospheric Science. He is director of the Bimini Biological Field Station, founder and a distinguished fellow of the American Elasmobranch Society, and has studied shark biology and behavior since 1961.

sharks differs from the other great group of fish-like vertebrates, the teleosts or bony fishes.

Sharks are an ancient group of vertebrates (backboned animals). They arose in the Paleozoic some 400,000,000 years ago during a period we call the Devonian. At that time, most of the recognizable invertebrates such as starfish, sea worms, jelly fish, clams, and crabs existed, but very few fishes could yet be found. Those that swam were like small jawless vacuum cleaners — primitive, armored things. There were, however, some larger, jawed fishes with articulated bones covering their bodies like medieval, aquatic knights. The fossil record shows that these first, archaic fishes had skeletons composed of true bone. But a few million years later, a new, very different, and much more recognizable fish-like vertebrate began to show up. Unlike their bony cousins, the skeletons of these fishes were completely cartilaginous and flexible. If you caught one of these eight-pound Devonian fishes, you would have no trouble recognizing it

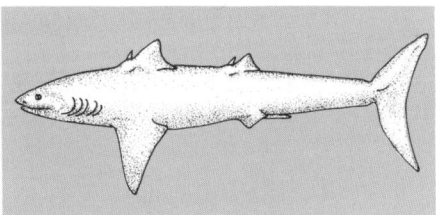

Primitive Devonian shark, Chladoselache sp. Drawing by M. Gruber.

as a kind of small primitive shark. Thus arose a new group of fishes, the Chondricthyes, which today comprise the sharks, skates, rays, sawfishes, and a strange group, the chimaeras. Over the next hundred million years, the Chondricthyes underwent extreme and often bizarre evolutionary experimentation with a variety of body-types, odd mating structures, and feeding specializations. In the Carboniferous, some 320-250 million years ago, sharks and their relatives passed through what Dick Lund calls their "Golden Age." (See Lund in this issue.) Swimming in the warm shallow seas of Montana along with another survivor from that dim age, the coelacanth, sharks actually outnumbered the bony fishes by a ratio of 6 to 4.

alone, as interpreted within life history theory, was to have profound implications on the evolution of sharks and set both biological — and for man — economic constraints on their abundance.

So what is it that we are talking about when we deal with life history? According to ecologists, an organism's life history is composed of patterns or episodes

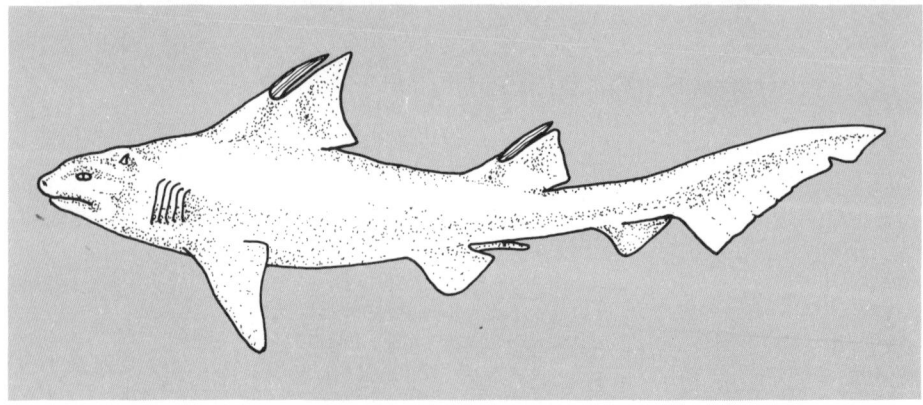

A Mesozoic littoral shark, Hybodus sp. Drawing by M. Gruber.

In addition to structural differences, studies have suggested that the cartilaginous fishes already possessed a lifestyle radically different from their less than numerous bony counterparts. Analyses of the fossil record yielded strong evidence that the basic pattern of shark life in the Carboniferous era was much the same as today. To biologists, the key to this insight is provided by a fin structure more characteristic of sharks than their jaws and teeth. Even the most ancient sharks possessed finger-like extensions of their pelvic (rearward paired) fins called "claspers." We know from modern sharks that these claspers are sex organs used by males during mating to impregnate females through copulation and internal fertilization. Thus, fully 350,000,000 years ago, sharks had evolved a reproductive strategy which favors the production of a small number of offspring, retained, protected, and nourished within the body of the mother, and requiring a strong investment of the female's time and resources. This fact

of growth, where the individual reaches maturity through a process known as differentiation, obtains and stores resources, and produces offspring. From a research viewpoint, the scientist collects data on growth, behavior, reproduction, and inheritance (genetics) to produce theories about how the course of evolution has adapted a particular species to its niche. The manifestation of this evolutionary course is called the "life history strategy" of a species. Here, strategy may be thought of as a set of inherited traits, molded by natural selection which allows an animal (or plant) to solve an ecological problem. Since all evolution depends upon "survival of the fittest," reproductive success plays a central role in life history theory. Simply put, in the game of life, an animal stakes its babies on a changeable and often unreliable world. The animal wins the game if its offspring survive to play another round of the game of life. The appropriate tactics for winning the game make up the successful life history strategy.

The crucial and practical question for us is whether the 400,000,000-year-old life history strategy of sharks will permit them to play another round of life in an ocean increasingly populated by super-predators plying the seas with mechanized fleets, freezer ships, 100-mile long lines and 30,000 miles of drifting gill nets. But more about that later.

Obviously, any life history is composed of a large number of biological variables, so the potential number of life history patterns is enormous. But this must be so. No two creatures can have exactly the same pattern or one would eventually out compete and destroy the other. Thus, when we speak of the "life history of sharks," it must be clear that we are talking about 350 different patterns corresponding to the 350 or so living species.

Within the sharks, there will be a range of variables which have evolved and represents a trade-off between the cost of developing that variable and the benefit of possessing it. For example, sheer size is one of the most obvious and readily appreciated characteristics of a species. The weight and length of living sharks varies through several orders of magnitude from a few ounces to many tons. On the one hand, the Pacific dwarf shark grows to a maximum length of less than 12 inches. On the other, the gigantic, filter-feeding, whale shark certainly reaches 45 feet and is the largest fish in the sea.

Benefits of large size include better offensive and defensive capacities. Elephants and large sharks have no natural enemies other than man. But it costs a lot to maintain a large body. This is what I mean by trade-offs. On the overall scale of animals, sharks may be considered large.

Growth and development are related to size and are very important as they affect the onset of maturity and ultimately reproduction. All kinds of growth patterns are found in nature. Many fishes go through a tiny larval stage where the flimsy individual looks nothing like its parent.

But most sharks follow a rather conventional pattern of growth and development. After a long period of fetal development from the egg — up to 22 months in the dogfish, even longer than an elephant — the shark pup is born in a large and advanced state. Most newborn sharks are miniatures of their parents and recognizable from the start.

After birth, the process of growth to maturity assumes an important role in life history theory. One strategy is to pour effort into rapid maturation so that the species can reproduce as fast as possible. Some insects require only hours after hatching to reach maturity, and the male neither feeds nor sleeps but functions only in sexual reproduction. Such animals are on a fast track. But this is definitely not the case for sharks. They are on a slow track. My studies of the lemon shark, a large, tropical predator, illustrate the general strategy followed by most of the familiar species.

Lemon sharks are born in the spring on shallow mangrove flats, fully formed and ready to go. The pups average two feet and a little over two pounds at birth. The mothers on the other hand are at least eight and a half feet long and around 350 pounds at first maturity. Thus a lemon shark pup must double its length and double it again, undergoing a simultaneous increase in mass of over 150-fold before it can reproduce. From our tagging studies we were very surprised to see how slowly lemon sharks grow. Most biologists believe that the pattern of growth in sharks follows the so-called VonBertalanffy model. According to this model, the most rapid growth occurs after birth, gradually slowing down as the animal ages until it just about stops after maturity. Thus the newborn shark is growing at the fastest rate just as is the newborn human infant. What was so surprising to us was that a two-foot lemon pup grows only 3-4 inches in its first year of life. Even if it grew a steady 4 inches per year, it would take over a decade to reach sexual maturity. In fact, lemon sharks require 13-15 years to become sexually active. Compare this strategy to that of the salmon which passes through several larval stages, migrates to the sea, undergoes long oceanic migrations, returns to its home stream, mates, lays 2000 fertile eggs, and dies all in the space of two years. Sharks are indeed on a slow-track.

Reproduction is really the central issue in life history studies and is the key to many of the evolutionary aspects of life history theory. Reproduction is a highly variable process ranging from asexual development where species such as corals simply form buds as one of the colonial animals, called polyps, divides in two, to sexual reproduction requiring the union of egg and sperm. All reproduction in sharks is sexual, but because they are a very ancient group, they display some of the most variable reproductive strategies of any vertebrate class. As you will read, there are sharks that lay eggs like chickens, sharks that retain eggs within their bodies like rattlesnakes, and sharks that develop from materials passed via the mother's blood through a placenta and umbilicus in a way perfectly analogous to the mammals. But even with all this variation, one thread unites the reproductive strategies of all sharks: fertilization is always internal and the shark mother produces a small number of well formed babies after a long period of development usually requiring a strong investment of

Nurse sharks mating. Photo by N. Rouse.

Birth of a lemon shark. Photo by R. Jureit.

her food resources. Added to this, many sharks require decades to reach maturity, then spend up to two years of pregnancy, and may mate only every other year. Lemon shark pups develop over a long 12 months of pregnancy, and the mothers require an additional 12 months to regenerate their bodies before mating again. Thus a mating pair of lemon sharks barely reproduce themselves over the 24-month reproductive cycle. Typically 8-12 pups are born every other year with a first year mortality approaching 50%. So from two mature sharks only 1-3 babies survive every third year. Clearly rebuilding a population under these circumstances would take many decades. And so it goes for the majority of sharks. There are some small species which are on a somewhat faster track such as the hound, tope, and sharpnose sharks. These mature relatively quickly in perhaps only two years and some species even reproduce annually through two seasons. But they still have a very low reproductive potential, giving birth in some cases to only 3-4 pups each season.

Many other factors such as longevity, migration and dispersal, energy storage, behavior as it relates to obtaining resources (food, space), and parental care all are sources of life history variability and provide the raw materials for evolution to mold a particular species to its niche. In addition to these individual life history variables, there are a number of composite factors such as age at maturity, frequency of reproduction and litter size, age at last reproduction, and rate of sur-

Lemon shark mother and baby. Photo by D. Perrine.

vival. Such factors can be combined into a so-called life table. Life tables are the basic tool of actuaries, the statisticians who determine how much your insurance premiums will cost. The life table gives actuarians information on whether the segment of the population you belong to is stable, shrinking, or growing; what the age distribution in your segment of the population is; and, most important, what the average chances of your survival are.

Fishery biologists do the same thing with life tables. While they do not bill the fish for insurance premiums, they nevertheless can have a profound effect on the fish's quality of life since they make recommendations to government managers which can keep a stock from being overfished. I will take up the question of overexploitation and management for sharks shortly. But first I would like to outline some of the theoretical aspects of life history theory as they relate to evolution and ecology.

In general the life pattern of sharks may be characterized by slow growth, delayed maturity, low fecundity combined with production of a few advanced offspring, longevity, multiple breeding, and large size. This pattern can be found in a number of terrestrial and marine creatures and represents one end of a scale of life history patterns. The other end might be illustrated by certain bony fish. As already mentioned the main features of a salmon's life history pattern include rapid growth, early maturity, high fecundity combined with the production of thousands of tiny, poorly developed, flimsy offspring, single breeding followed by death: in other words, a short, fast life cycle. Biologists studying various life histories recognized this apparent dichotomy many years ago. In 1958 after years of study, the famous ecologist, Robert McArthur, was able to explain the significance of these two ongoing patterns. McArthur knew that the ground work for describing how a particular population grows or declines was formulated two centuries ago when Malthus predicted that humans would eventually overpopulate the world. Sixty years ago the mathematician Lotka refined the original work and produced a mathematical model of population growth which is used today by most ecologists. Lotka realized that for animals and humans living under constant and favorable conditions the population will tend to stabilize. Increases due to new births are exactly offset by deaths. Such a population has a stable age distribution and is said to be in equilibrium. Now imagine that a sudden catastrophe kills off a large number of individuals. Clearly, the population will rebound if conditions after the disaster are restored. If this were not the case, each catastrophic event would push the population ever closer to extinction.

With fewer mouths to feed after the event, a survivor might have an easier time finding food which would provide more time for successful breeding. So as conditions improve over time, more and more parents will be having more and more babies. Thus in a favorable and uncrowded environment with unlimited resources, the numbers would gather speed then explode. The analytical expression for such an explosion is called an exponential curve. However, a time will come when the habitat again gets crowded, resources will begin to limit the behavior of the individual, and the environment will be carrying about as many animals as possible. As this happens, population growth declines until once again the number of births and deaths will stabilize. This situation is analogous to placing a fund in a savings bank and allowing it to grow with compound interest. At some point the depositor begins to withdraw the interest but leaves the principal intact. The overall mathematical expression describing both the population and bank account is an S-shaped graph of numbers (dollars) over time. This is called a logistical curve.

Now consider a species that lives in an unstable and unpredictable environment such as a rocky shoreline where the vagaries of both terrestrial and aquatic conditions conspire to cause frequent catastrophes. Such a species must have a life style adapted to these disasters and be able to quickly take advantage of new and uncrowded conditions. Consider on the other hand a different species living under constant conditions in a very stable environment such as the deep sea where the sun never shines and the temperature doesn't vary more than a few degrees.

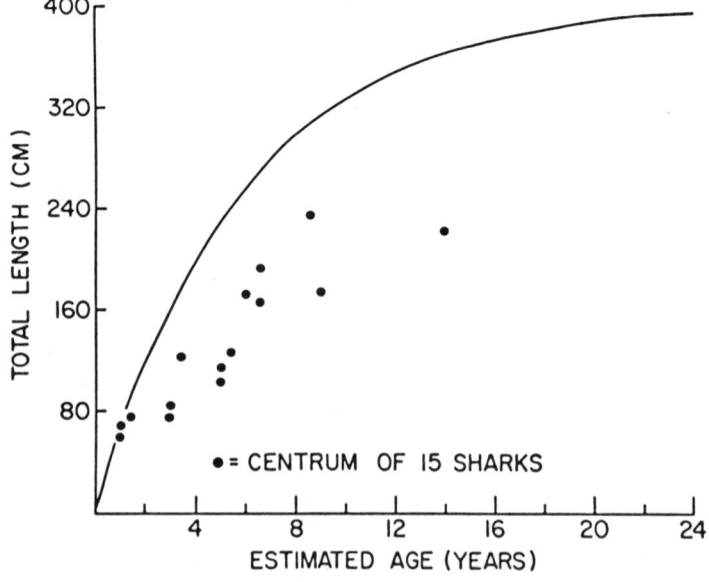

Relationship between the theoretical VonBertalanffy growth model (smooth curve) and estimated age-at-length of lemon sharks (solid circles).

Spiny dogfish. Photo by J. Stafford-Deitsch.

Such an animal must be adapted to withstand competition and predation, find and process food efficiently, and generally be prepared to live under conditions approaching the ability of the environment to support or "carry" its kind. McArthur called the former species "r-Selected" and the latter "K-Selected," after the constants in Lotka's formula for population growth.

The theory of r/K selection has been with us for three decades and has its adherents and opponents. Its appeal lies in its ease of understanding, and especially in the framework it provides for judging the life history pattern of a species and how that pattern relates to the ecology and evolution of an animal. The framework allows us to list the traits of a species life history and predict more or less how its life history strategy evolved.

So, what does the theory or r/K selection predict, and how do sharks fit in? First, where adult mortality is high compared to that of juveniles, single breeding is favored...as with the salmon. In contrast, low fecundity combined with high juvenile mortality would tend to favor repeated breeding as is found for sharks. The rationale here is literally why put all your eggs in one basket. Another prediction involves age at first reproduction: Expanding populations will have a lower age at maturity; stable or declining populations will have delayed maturity especially when increased size, age, or social status favors reproductive success. Such is the case for sharks. There is some evidence that dogfish sharks making a comeback from overfishing in the North Sea are maturing at a somewhat earlier age than virgin dogfish stocks. But, by and large, sharks mature very slowly.

We can predict that increased predation will favor large offspring while increased resources favor smaller ones. For the lemon shark the most critical time is the first year when competition and predation is high. Only about half the lemon shark pups survive the first year because competition and predation are high. But as they grow, their chances for survival increase to a point where there would be very few predators, other than man, that could kill a six-foot lemon shark.

So, growing populations are characterized by early maturity, early and strong reproductive effort, and large brood size. Animals adapted to a fluctuating or r-selected environment should be small, mature quickly, mate early, and produce a herd of tiny offspring with little or no parental care but with a major reproductive effort and low survivorship as an adult.

In contrast, animals such as sharks, adapted to a stable or K-selecting environment can be expected to grow slowly to a large size, mature late in life, reproduce seasonally, (year after year), producing a few, large babies which receive parental care (in the case of sharks, during pregnancy only), and have a good survival rate as adults. Thus in all respects, sharks may be considered the architypical K-selected species. Considering the geological age of the sharks, they may have been the first vertebrate group to take up (evolve) the K-selected lifestyle.

But these are theoretical concepts. From a more practical viewpoint how does the shark's K-selected life strategy serve them today? Two factors that are characteristic of animals with K-selected life-history strategies are (1) that the habitat they occupy must be relatively stable with respect to resources and conditions, and (2) that competition and predation, especially on the adults is relatively low. Both of these requirements have been severely disturbed in recent years due to the activity of man. No more are many of the habitats of sharks stable, benign places. For instance, sharks often give birth in special inshore areas of high productivity known as nursery grounds where the pups spend up to several years of their most sensitive period. But beachfront development and wetland industrialization has seriously impacted this critical environment with oil spills, chemical pollution, and physical degradation. Added to this, man, the super-predator, is not only out-competing sharks for food with mechanized killer fleets and drifting death nets, but taking sharks themselves at ever increasing rates. Clearly the requirements of stable conditions, ample resources, and low predation in many cases no longer hold. This, combined with the low fecundity and slow growth of the (K-selected) sharks, has put them in the trouble we see today. The hammering that sharks stocks are taking simply cannot be sustained. So, the 400,000,000-year-old K-selected life history strategy, so successful for sharks — as well as sea turtles and whales — has today placed them in jeopardy. As you will read in several articles in this volume, an ever increasing awareness of the importance of sharks to the overall health of the oceans and a more enlightened understanding of sharks in general has led conservation groups to take up the plight of the cartilaginous fishes. Now the U.S. Government recognizes the role of sharks and is moving, albeit slowly, to protect them. We can only hope that you, our concerned readers will support the growing movement to stop the killing and restore the shark to its previously successful, K-selected life style.

ADDITIONAL READING:

Honig, John and S.H. Gruber. 1990 In Press. Life history patterns in the elasmobranchs. U.S. Dept. of Commerce, NOAA Tech. Rpt. NMFS.

Horn, Henry. 1884. Optimal tactics of reproduction and life history. Ch. 14, pp. 412-429. In: Krebs, E. and N. Davies (eds.). Behavioral Ecology: An Evolutionary Approach. Blackwell Scientific Publ., Oxford.

McArthur, Robert and E.O. Wilson. 1967. THE THEORY OF ISLAND BIOGEOGRAPHY. Princeton University Press, Princeton, NJ. 203 pp.

Stearns, Stephen. 1976. Life history tactics: A review of the ideas. Quart. Rev. Biol. 51(1):3-47.

Sharpnose shark. Photo by D. Perrine.

The Evolution and Diversity of Sharks

By LEONARD J.V. COMPAGNO

Classification of Sharklike Fishes

The classification of the major groups of sharklike fishes will be treated only broadly here as befits the nature of this essay. The relationships of the sharklike fishes, Class Chondrichthyes, to other classes of jawed fishes is still debated by evolutionary biologists, as is the validity of the Chondrichthyes as a monophyletic group. Most modern researchers accept the Class Chondrichthyes although some hold for a phyletic relationship of the chimaeroids (Holocephalii) with the chimaeroid-like Ptyctodontiformes in the Class Placodermi, and a phyletic relationship of the sharks and rays (Elasmobranchii) with other groups of placoderms, with the spiny-finned fishes, Class Acanthodii, or with the bony fishes, Class Osteichthyes.

The classification of cartilaginous fishes presented here follows my earlier work on living sharks and other elasmobranchs, while the research of Zangerl, Cappetta, and Carroll is followed in part for fossil cartilaginous fishes. There is little agreement at present on the classification, composition, and interrelationships of early groups of cartilaginous fishes or of the interrelationships of living shark and ray groups. As a consequence I use the following phenetic classification of living and fossil cartilaginous fishes, which is a simplified and conservative working arrangement.

Compagno is curator of fishes and directs the Shark Research Center at the South African Museum, Cape Town. A native Californian, he was a founding member of the American Elasmobranch Society, is a member of the International Working Group on Cartilaginous Fishes, senior editor of Chondros, *and author of the* FAO CATALOGUE OF WORLD SHARKS.

Class Chondrichthyes:
  Cartilaginous fishes.
Subclass Elasmobranchii:
  Sharklike fishes.
Cohort Palaeoselachii (Cladoselachii, Pleuropterygii):
  Archaic Paleozoic sharks.
Order Cladoselachiformes:
  Cladoselachian sharks.
Order Coronodontiformes:
  Coronodont sharks.
Order Desmiodontiformes:
  Desmiodont sharks.
Order Symmoriiformes:
  Symmorioid sharks.
Order Edestiformes (Eugeneodontida): Edestoid sharks.
Order Orodontiformes:
  Orodont sharks.
Order Petalodontiformes:
  Petalodonts.
Order Squatinactiformes:
  Squatinactids.
Cohort Euselachii:
  Ctenacanth, hybodont, xenacanth, and modern sharks.
Subcohort Protoselachii: Ctenacanth, hybodont, and xenacanth sharks.
Order Ctenacanthiformes:
  Ctenacanth sharks.
Order Xenacanthiformes:
  Xenacanth sharks.
Order Hybodontiformes:
  Hybodont sharks.
Subcohort Neoselachii:
  Modern sharks and rays.
Superorder Palaeospinacomorphii:
  Early neoselachians.
Order Palaeospinaciforms:
  Early neoselachians.
Superorder Squalomorphii:
  Squalomorph sharks.
Order Hexanchiformes:
  Cow and frilled sharks.

Order Squaliformes:
    Dogfish sharks.
Order Pristiophoriformes:
    Sawsharks.
Order Protospinaciformes:
    Shark-rays.
Superorder Squatinomorphii:
    Angel sharks.
Order Squatiniformes:
    Angel sharks.
Superorder Rajomorphii (Batoidea):
    Rays.
Order Pristiformes: Sawfish.
Order Rhinobatiformes:
    Guitarfishes.
Order Torpediniformes:
    Electric rays.
Order Rajiformes: Skates.
Order Myliobatiformes: Stingrays.
Superorder Galeomorphii:
    Galeomorph sharks.
Order Heterodontiformes:
    Bullhead sharks.
Order Orectolobiformes:
    Carpet sharks.
Order Lamniformes:
    Mackerel sharks.
Order Carcharhiniformes:
    Ground sharks.
Subclass Holocephalii
    (Subterbranchialia): Chimaeroids.

**Evolutionary Patterns
of Sharks and Other
Cartilaginous Fishes.**

The fossil record of chondrichthyans is vexingly imperfect, in part because the cartilaginous skeletons of sharklike fishes are well-preserved as fossils only in the most exceptional circumstances. Teeth, fin spines, and dermal denticles and their derivatives are often the only fossilized remains in cartilaginous fishes. These can be very difficult to interpret, particularly because of individual, ontogenetic, sexual, and positional variation and also because of conservatism in structure that may not be reflected in other organs. Thus the fossil record affords only a partial glimpse of the complex and broad evolution pattern of sharklike fishes.

Chondrichthyan evolution can be divided into three stages, punctuated by major extinctions among cartilaginous fishes and other aquatic organisms. The first Paleozoic stage was a massive basal adaptive radiation during the Devonian and Carboniferous that included the bifurcation of shark (elasmobranchs) and chimaeroid (holocephalian) subclasses; the proliferation of various groups of archaic sharks (palaeoselachians), euselachian sharks including the first neoselachians; and the culmination of chimaeroid evolution. This was truncated by the extinction of palaeoselachian sharks and decimation of protoselachian sharks and chimaeroids during the Permian-Triassic transition.

The second Mesozoic stage saw the protoselachian hybodont sharks and chimaeroids each undergoing a secondary radiation which was greatly overshadowed by the large adaptive radiation in the mid-Mesozoic of the neoselachians, including modern sharks and the first batoids. The Cretaceous-Paleocene transition saw the extinction of the last protoselachians, a decrease in diversity of chimaeroids, and the survival of most or all groups of neoselachians with considerable loss of diversity.

The third Cenozoic stage saw a reshuffling of the diversity of neoselachian sharks with the carcharhinoids eventually achieving dominance over other orders of living sharks. Two of the most derived batoid groups, the more speciose but more conservative rajoids (skates) and the more morphologically varied, progressive myliobatoids (stingrays), rose to preeminence in taxonomic and ecological diversity compared to less derived ray groups, thus showing the shift from the early primacy of palaeoselachians, protoselachians, and chimaeroids in the Paleozoic, to the dominance of neoselachians at present.

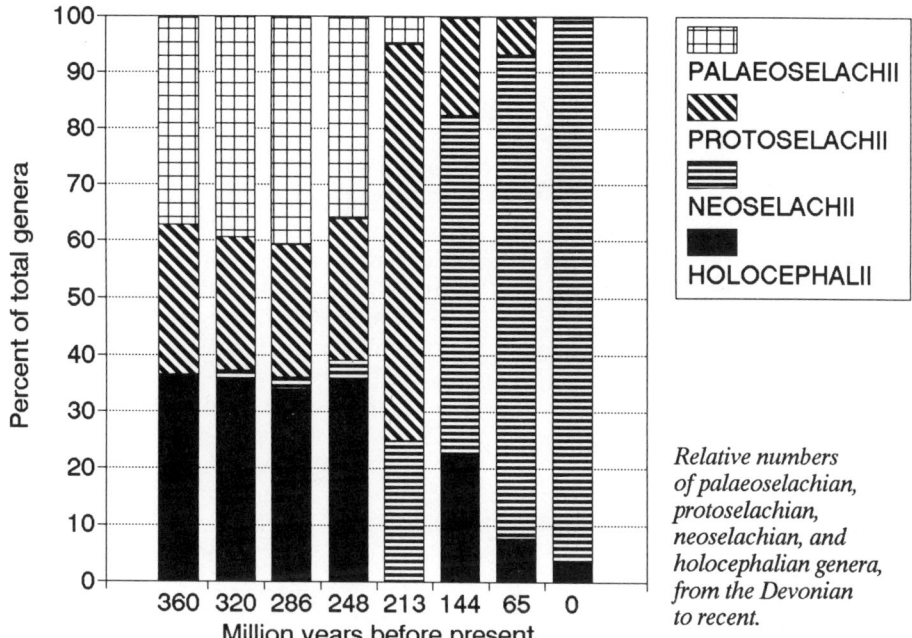

Relative numbers of palaeoselachian, protoselachian, neoselachian, and holocephalian genera, from the Devonian to recent.

Diversity of Modern Sharks and Their Relatives

Living sharks and their relatives are a highly successful group of aquatic vertebrates, apparently quite competitive in marine, large-predator, and bottom-feeder niches. Garrick and Compagno reviewed the diversity of living sharks and other cartilaginous fishes from a taxonomic perspective, while elsewhere I have dealt with the ecological and morphological diversity of modern cartilaginous fishes. Table 1 is a listing of numbers of living cartilaginous fishes, taken from a computer database and updated from the numbers previously presented in my papers and books, for various shark and ray groups. It contains estimates for the numbers of families, genera, and species of living cartilaginous fishes current to May 1990. The maximum listings for species include estimates of numbers of undescribed taxa known to me, particularly in the Indian Ocean and around Australia, as well as dubious species that may not be valid and are not included in the counts of recognized species.

The modern cartilaginous fishes may comprise between 900 and 1100 known species, and includes approximately 168 genera and 51 families. Chimaeras include less than 6% of the families, genera, and species of living chondrichthyans, and although sufficiently abundant in some localities to support small-scale fisheries, are clearly a minor group compared to neoselachian sharks and rays. Living sharks are more diverse than rays in higher taxa but have fewer species. Rays have approximately 60% of the families and genera of sharks, but about 131% of the species. Ray genera average 8.1 species per genus while shark genera average 3.7 species.

Differences in diversity at the familial and generic level can be seen in the various orders of living chondrichthyans. Diversity indices were calculated for each order as average numbers of genera per family (genus diversity index) and average numbers of species per genus (species diversity index), and plotted for

Table 1. Numbers of families, genera, and species of living sharks, rays, and chimaeras, estimates as of May 2, 1990. For species in each group a MINimum and MAXimum figure and percentages are given. Minimums represent a close estimate of valid described species and maximums include dubious species and undescribed species known to the author.

1. SHARK GROUPS AS PERCENT TOTAL SHARKS:

| | FAMILIES | | GENERA | | SPECIES | | | |
| | | | | | MIN | | MAX | |
	NO.	%	NO.	%	NO.	%	NO.	%
Cow & Frilled Sharks	2	6.7	4	4.0	5	1.3	5	1.0
Dogfish Sharks	3	10.0	21	20.8	88	23.4	109	22.7
Saw Sharks	1	3.3	2	2.0	5	1.3	9	1.9
Angel Sharks	1	3.3	1	1.0	13	3.5	17	3.5
Bullhead Sharks	1	3.3	1	1.0	8	2.1	10	2.1
Carpet Sharks	7	23.3	14	13.9	32	8.5	35	7.3
Mackerel Sharks	7	23.3	10	9.9	15	4.0	16	3.3
Ground Sharks	8	26.7	48	47.5	210	55.9	280	58.2
Total Sharks	30		101		376		481	

2. RAY GROUPS AS PERCENT TOTAL RAYS:

| | FAMILIES | | GENERA | | SPECIES | | | |
| | | | | | MIN | | MAX | |
ORDER:	NO.	%	NO.	%	NO.	%	NO.	%
Guitarfishes	3	16.7	9	14.8	53	10.7	61	10.7
Sawfishes	1	5.6	2	3.3	4	0.8	5	0.9
Electric Rays	4	22.2	11	18.0	43	8.7	57	10.0
Skates	2	11.1	17	27.9	225	45.5	262	45.9
Stingrays	8	44.4	22	36.1	169	34.2	186	32.6
Total Rays	18		61	36.3	494	54.8	571	51.8

3. SHARKS, RAYS AND CHIMAERAS AS PERCENT TOTALS OF ALL LIVING CARTILAGINOUS FISHES:

| | FAMILIES | | GENERA | | SPECIES | | | |
| | | | | | MIN | | MAX | |
GROUP:	NO.	%	NO.	%	NO.	%	NO.	%
Sharks	30	58.8	101	60.1	376	41.7	481	43.6
Rays	18	35.3	61	36.3	494	54.8	571	51.8
Total Sharks & Rays	48	94.1	162	96.4	870	96.6	1052	95.5
Chimaeras	3	5.9	6	3.6	31	3.4	50	4.5
Total Cartilaginous Fishes	51		168		901		1102	

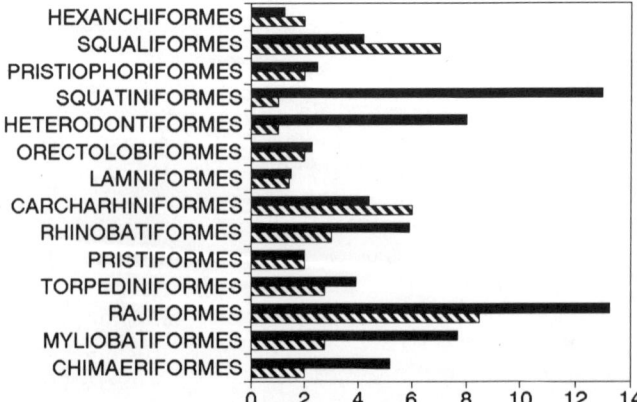

Diversity indices for the orders of living sharks, rays, and chimaeras. These include average number of species per genera (black), and average number of genera per family for each order.

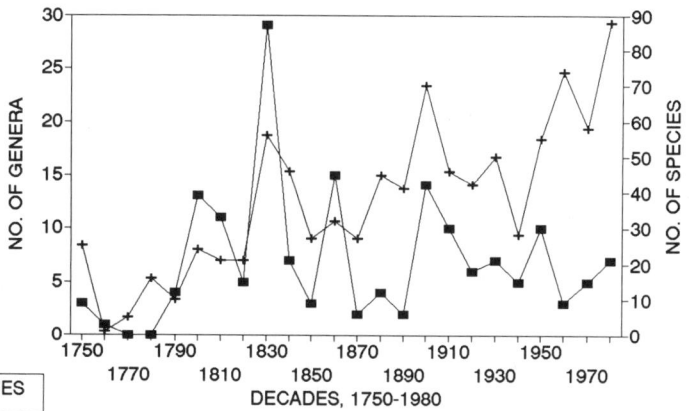

Numbers of currently recognized, valid genera and species of cartilaginous fishes described per decade over the past 240 years.

each order. The hexanchoids, pristiophoroids, orectoloboids, lamnoids, and pristoids have low genus and species indices, while the squaloids and carcharhinoids have high genus indices and moderately high species indices. The squatinoids and heterodontoids have high species indices but low generic indices, while the rajoids have very high genus and species indices. Other orders are intermediate. Judging from the fossil record and from current patterns of diversity, the orders with low genus and species indices are for the most part groups past their evolutionary prime, and were formerly far more diverse than they are today. The orders with high genus and species indices are currently dominant in diversity and were less diverse in the past, while those with low genus and high species diversity are minor groups that never were dominant.

Description of new species of cartilaginous fishes occurs at the relatively high rate of approximately ten species a year, of which between a third and half are sharks. A plot of numbers of currently recognized genera and species of cartilaginous fishes described per decade for the past 240 years suggests that while valid genera have been described at an irregularly decreasing rate in the last 50 years, there has been a marked increase in species descriptions during the same time. It suggests that there will be many new species to be discovered in the future but fewer taxa at the generic level and probably also at higher taxa level. In other words, we now have a reasonably good picture of the current diversity of living cartilaginous fishes despite disagreements on their interrclationships and classification, and we continue to discover new species.

In the future there may be fewer major discoveries of higher taxa of cartilaginous fishes such as the megamouth sharks (Megachasmidae) and sixgill stingrays (Hexatrygonidae). Presumably nothing comparable to the discovery of the living coelacanth will occur among cartilaginous fishes (such as the location of surviving palaeoselachians, protoselachians, or archaic chimaeroids), but I hope I'll be proved wrong on this. However, as exploration of poorly known marine habitats continues, there may not be a corresponding decrease in the description of new species of cartilaginous fishes for several decades. The number of valid species may very well exceed 1200 in the next century. In contrast, regarding fossil cartilaginous fishes, particularly Paleozoic groups, we may be viewing only a hint of the taxonomic diversity at all levels.

Most species of living cartilaginous fishes are concentrated on the world's continental and insular shelves and adjacent slopes. Approximately 5% of known cartilaginous fishes are oceanic (mostly sharks), while about 50% are on the shelves from the seashore to 200 m (650 ft). About 5% occur in fresh water, about 35% occur on the slopes from 200 to 2000 m and occasionally deeper, and about 5% occur on the shelves and slopes, on the shelves and oceanically, or in all three habitats. Chondrichthyan faunas of the temperate shelves are perhaps the best known, especially in the Northern Hemisphere. Tropical shelf faunas, particularly from the west-central Indian Ocean east to the Indo-Australian Archipelago, are less well known and in recent years have yielded a number of new species.

Freshwater chondrichthyans are few compared to teleosts but include a handful of euryhaline carcharhinid sharks and pristids and a fair variety of obligate tropical freshwater stingrays. The chondrichthyan faunas of the continental slopes are best known in the North Atlantic and to a lesser extent off Japan, the Eastern North Pacific, Australia, and New Zealand. Knowledge of slope cartilaginous fishes ranges from unsatisfactory to almost nothing, and new species, occasional new genera, and range extensions for described species are regularly reported. Oceanic cartilaginous fishes have low diversity, but occasional new species, genera, and even families (megamouth shark, Megachasmidae), have been discovered in recent years. Cartilaginous fishes of shelf, slope, and oceanic habitats are least diverse at high latitudes and most varied in warm temperate seas and in the tropics.

I can attempt to project from past performance in the last few decades the potential yield of new species from various chondrichthyan groups. Of the eight orders and 30 families of living sharks, some are yielding few new species while others are "growth groups" that regularly deliver new taxa. The hexanchoids, pristiophoroids, squatinoids, and heterodontoids have few living taxa and perhaps relatively few to be discovered, but the squaloids, with most species on the deep slopes and with a sizable oceanic component, present a regular trickle of new species and sometimes new genera. The lamnoids and orectoloboids now have few living species, many of which were described in the eighteenth and nineteenth centuries and might have low potential for further growth, but one should take note that 27% of the lamnoid species and 16% of the orectoloboids were described in the last five decades. The dominant carcharhinoids may have few new species of carcharhinids, sphyrnids, hemigaleids, leptochariids, pseudotriakids, and proscylliids to contribute in the future, but the triakids and especially the scyliorhinids are "growth groups," particularly in outer shelf and slope genera. As shown by Stewart Springer's revision of the scyliorhinids and subsequent publications by various authors, this highly diverse family will probably continue to yield new species at a reasonable rate.

Of the five orders of batoids, the inshore pristoids may yield few if any new species in the future, but growth is anticipated among the primarily shelf-dwelling rhinobatoids, torpedinoids, and myliobatoids, particularly in the tropical Indo-West Pacific. Additional species of freshwater myliobatoid stingrays may be discovered, particularly in Asia and South America. The rajoids continue as the principal growth group among batoids, and new skates stream in at an impressive rate. The chimaeroids are primarily deep-water chondrichthyans, and one can anticipate moderate species growth in slope chimaerids and possibly rhinochimaerids, but little if any in the shelf callorhinchids.

Shark Diversity and Conservation

A problem in studying the diversity of living sharks and other cartilaginous fishes is that sharks may possibly be decreasing in various habitats because of human activities. Particularly worrisome are inshore and freshwater habitats in the tropics, which burgeoning human populations are increasingly exploiting for food; the oceanic habitat, where epipelagic elasmobranchs have been hammered in international pelagic longline and gillnet fisheries; and the upper slopes, where deep bottom-trawl fisheries are operating internationally and exploiting poorly-known faunas. Expanding fisheries have outstepped knowledge of the diversity and distribution of cartilaginous fishes, and in some instances may be threatening the survival of undescribed and poorly known species as well as more familar cartilaginous fishes.

It is heartening that, with the general awareness of the human threat to ecological diversity in scientific and popular circles, some international researchers of sharks and other cartilaginous fishes have focused on the particular vulnerability of these fishes to overexploitation. The American Elasmobranch Society has recently shown considerable interest in chondrichthyan conservation. There are groups working on this issue in the United Kingdom and Australia, and *Chondros*, an international newsletter directed to chondrichthyan conservation, has recently been launched. I would like to be less pessimistic, but those of us in the chondrichthyan research community who are concerned with conservation may very well be in the position of very small mice seeking to bell a very large cat. A great idea, chondrichthyan conservation, but, how, in the face of the ecocidal monster that grinds down the diversity of life at all levels, does one accomplish it?

If it doesn't happen, we may very well face an end to the unfolding story of the diversity of living sharklike fishes. These animals might be represented partly or entirely in museum specimens. The once-living species might then be equivalent to the fossil chondrichthyans, and can join the ranks of palaeoselachians as well as the great auk, dodo, and the passenger pigeon. The potential ecological damage resulting from the decimation or removal

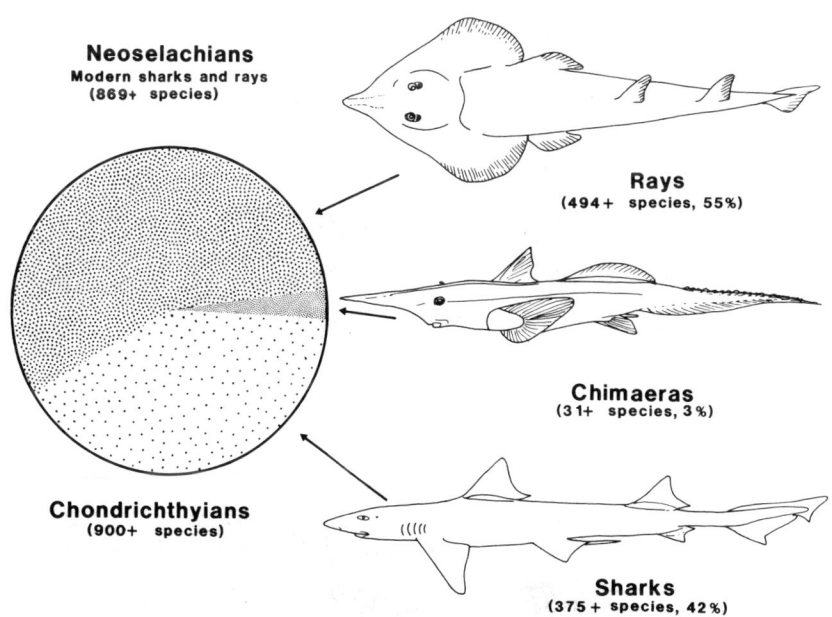

Numbers of species of living Chondrichthyes and percentages of sharks, rays, and chimaeras. Numbers are minimum estimates counted as of May 1, 1989.

of an important group of high-level predators such as the sharklike fishes is incalculable. For people such as Stewart Springer and others of us who have devoted their research careers to studying chondrichthyan diversity, this is not a prospect to treasure.

Note: Stewart Springer, one of the most important figures in shark biology of the mid and late twentieth century, figured strongly in the initial stages of my predoctoral work at Stanford University during the mid-1960s. He headed a small Bureau of Commercial Fisheries laboratory housed in the basement of the east wing of the Stanford Museum. This was by far the leading center for graduate research in systematic ichthyology in the United States with outstanding researchers from the earliest days under David Starr Jordon, to my major professor, the late George Sprague Myers. There was also an excellent collection of shark specimens at Stanford and in the George Vanderbilt Foundation collections, a superb ichthyological library, and a vital research group of ichthyological faculty and graduate students. Stew was exceptionally friendly, interested, and generous in sharing his knowledge and the resources of his laboratory. His influence on my work was considerable. With much gratitude I dedicate this brief overview to Stewart Springer, who has done so much to explicate the diversity and biology of living sharks.

In addition I want to thank Dr. Samuel H. Gruber for inviting me to participate in this volume; the members of the shark Research Center; the Department of Marine Biology and the Director of the South African Museum for research support; the Foundation for Research Development for funding; and my wife, Martina Compagno Roeleveld, for support.

ADDITIONAL READING:

Cappetta, H. 1987. Chondrichthyes II. Mesozoic and Cenozoic Elasmobranchii. Pp. 1-193. In H.-P. Schultze (ed.) Handbook of Paleoichthyology vol. 3B, Gustav Fischer Verlag, Stuttgart.

Carroll, R.L. 1988. Vertebrate paleontology and evolution. W.H. Freeman, New York, iv, 698 pp.

Compagno, L.J.V. 1981. Legend versus reality: the Jaws image and shark diversity. Oceanus, 24(4):5-16.

1984. FAO Species Catalogue. Vol. 4, SHARKS OF THE WORLD.

FAO Fish. Syn. (125), 4(1):i-viii, 1-250; 4(2):i-x, 251-655.

1990. Alternate life history styles of cartilaginous fishes in time and space. Environm. Biol. Fishes.

Garrick, J.A.F. 1955. The diveristy of the shark world. Tuatara, 6(1):13-18.

Stevens, John D. (ed.) 1987. SHARKS. Golden Press Pty. Ltd., Australia, pp. 1-240.

Zangerl, R. 1981. Chondrichthyes I. Paleozoic Elasmobranchii. Pp. 1-115. In H.-P. Schultze (ed.) Handbook of Paleoichthyology vol. 3A. Gustav Fischer Verlag, Stuttgart.

Whale shark. Photo by J. Stafford-Deitsch.

Shadows in Time –
A Capsule History of Sharks

by RICHARD LUND

Sharks are creatures of mystery. They capture the imagination and are surrounded by myths that fill the broad gaps in our knowledge. They are elusive and notoriously hard to study in their natural habits. They are feared "eating machines," and folklore claims they have not changed in hundreds of millions of years.

Today's white shark is clearly one of the largest and most awesome marine predators, but 15 million-year-old fossil white shark teeth measuring up to nine inches along the cutting edge are relatively abundant. Size estimates of those white sharks range in the order of 40 feet, virtually defying the imagination. Just as the life history of many modern-day sharks remains elusive, little is known and less understood about the evolutionary history of sharks and the group to which they belong.

Since I will use the term in several different ways, let us understand what we are talking about when we call something a shark. Of course, the first image is conjured up by the first paragraph — fusiform fish with mobile and protrusible jaws containing many generations of replacement teeth, several separate external gill openings, skin covered with sharp-crested scales, and an upswept tail. Shark skeletons lack bones; their cartilage is stiffened by the same mineral deposits found in bone, but the deposits are laid down chiefly on the surfaces and chiefly in a pattern of barely visible polygonal prisms. Finally, sharks have internal fertilization, with the pelvic fins of male sharks bearing claspers to accomplish the necessary copulation. Skates and rays share the same unique features with sharks, but are easily distinguished because they have flattened bodies and expanded pectoral fins. So, sharks, skates, and rays are placed in the same group, the Elasmobranchii or strap-gills. I'll also call this larger group sharks.

A chimaera, according to my unabridged dictionary, can be one of four things: a fire-breathing monster composed of miscellaneous parts of goat, lion, and serpent; any similar fabulous monster; an impossible or idle fancy; or a particular group of cartilaginous fishes. The alternative definitions give one a slight idea that chimaeras (the fishes) might be somewhat problematical, and indeed they are. The nature of their skeleton allies them with sharks, as do the claspers, but there the resemblance stops. Their upper jaws are an immovable part of the braincase, they have evergrowing cutting or crushing plates on their jaws rather than teeth, and they have a single flap covering the gills, not separate slits. Oh yes, male chimaeras have some extraordinary gadgets, presumably to aid in copulation, but no one has seen much of living chimaera activities, and few people have succeeded in keeping them alive in captivity. The relationships of the chimaeras have been chimerical for almost two centuries. Are they and sharks related? If so, then how? The sharks, skates, rays, and chimaeras are usually put into one large group, the cartilaginous fish, which implies acceptance of a relationship. For the sake of space, I'll also call this group sharks.

The fossil record of any shark is poor.

Lund is a professor of biology at Adelphi University, Garden City, NY, and holds research appointments with the Carnegie Museum of Natural History and the Royal Ontario Museum. He has been excavating the Bear Gulch Limestones for 22 years.

Their cartilaginous skeletons and intrinsic rarity conspire to leave mostly isolated teeth, scales, or fin spines rather than whole animals that might tell us something more useful. Nevertheless, some interesting finds have been made through the years that allow us to determine something of their history and pathway through time. The earliest records occur very early in the history of animals with jaws, about 400 million years ago. The fossils consist of isolated scales that closely resemble those of today's sharks, but also closely resemble the scales of a bunch of jawless fish called thelodonts. We do not know whether this resemblance means a relationship or an evolutionary coincidence, and we know nothing further about the bearers of these scales. Speculatively, *if* these scales are shark scales, and *if* there is a relationship, this could mean that the ancestors of the sharks were also the ancestral group from which all other jawed fish, land vertebrates, and you and I derived.

Gavin Young plucked the next shreds of information from the side of a mountain in Antarctica, in Devonian-age rocks, about 15 million years younger. He found most of a small shark, with teeth, braincase, and complete scale covering. The rocks were from a fresh-water deposit, and the teeth were two-cusped upon a rather flat base. Variations on this tooth design would recur in fresh-water deposits throughout the world for almost 200 million years. These xenacanth sharks were a singularly successful, and highly predatory group. But no one could consider this earliest shark either primitive or an acceptable ancestral form for any later sharks, except for other xenacanths. And what were they doing in fresh water so early in the evolutionary game? Gavin Young has also found some provocative isolated shark teeth from around the same time, and these teeth are quite like those of modern mackerel sharks. They are not lamnid shark teeth, but we have no idea what sort of shark bore these teeth. There are no data on any other shark teeth resembling these until the later days of the dinosaurs.

Cleveland, Ohio, is built on the remnants of an old Devonian sea, back during the times that the Appalachians were a vigorous, up-and-coming mountain range. Also at this time, the first known four-footed amphibians left footprints, and the seas as well as rivers were alive with a variety of fishes that evolved from those first, unknown, jawed ancestors. Sharks were not the largest predators in the waters around Cleveland but rather the huge placoderm fish with their heavily armored heads and shoulders. Here, in Germany, and elsewhere, we can recognize several types of sharks, and remark upon some of their features. Their basic form is similar to today's sharks, but the body form of sharks has the deceptive simplicity of a hydrodynamically efficient, highly evolved predator. The scales of those that had not eliminated scales though some evolutionary specialization are of a simple design, apparently primitive but serving a streamlining function — a design concept copied by the winner of a recent America's Cup sailing competition. The use of stiffened cartilage, rather than heavy bony skeleton, saves a great deal of weight, and therefore swimming energy. The separate gill openings might be a bit harder to rationalize in energetic terms, but whatever function they serve seems to have been copied by the designers of modern hunter-killer nuclear submarines.

Teeth and tails are already highly varied in these Devonian cartilaginous fish; teeth are the aspects of food-getting that are most sensitive to evolutionary pressures, and tails are equally sensitive measures of swimming adaptations. It is no coincidence that one of the more famous Cleveland Shale sharks, *Cladoselache*, has a high energy tail closely resembling those of today's tuna and mackerels, rather than the tails of today's more "primitive"-looking sharks. With jaws full of sharp, pointed teeth and completely stripped-down and streamlined bodies, the sharks at the close of the Devonian had arrived at a body plan that is extremely easy to recognize today, that of efficiency through simplicity.

The end of the Devonian period was one of the most revolutionary times in the history of life on Earth. Among the many and dramatic changes that affected all those influences collectively known as natural selection was the complete and sudden extinction of the dominant, armor-bearing placoderm fish. Changes in mountain range, seaway and continent location, climate, and in life out of the water, all rendered the beginnings of the Carboniferous a very different scene from that which came before. At the risk of possible oversimplification, even the buckets of strange teeth that can be gathered from the early Carboniferous rocks in the midcontinental United States tell a story of dramatic changes in the players. We no longer find only multicuspid, sharp-pointed shark teeth, but multitudes of strange shapes composed of new and different microstructural arrangements of calcium phosphate minerals. Teeth are accompanied in the fossilized muds of these old waterways by dental plates that were probably retained for the lifetime of the bearers. Recently a window opened into this time, to allow us a tantalizing look at some of the sharks that left such quantities of curious, disembodied hard parts. This time window opened into a shallow, tropical bay, 320 million years ago, in what is now the Bear Gulch Limestones of central Montana.

What we see in the Bear Gulch Bay are sharks, in a variety of body forms, dental forms, and reproductive strategies, that clearly mark them as the most dominant and diverse vertebrates in the water — as if evolution had resulted in an explosion of experiments to fit the new ecological circumstances. Sharks were rare before, but here they made up 60% of the species of fish. Simple before, here they showed up in every conceivable form, and probably in every conceivable color combination. From unquestionably dominant apex predators, like the estimated 9-to-11-foot *Stethacanthus productus*, to the diminutive *Heteropetalus elegantulus*, and the strange *Belantsea montana*, sharks were everywhere. It is remarkable that while the large predators looked like we expect sharks to look, mature males

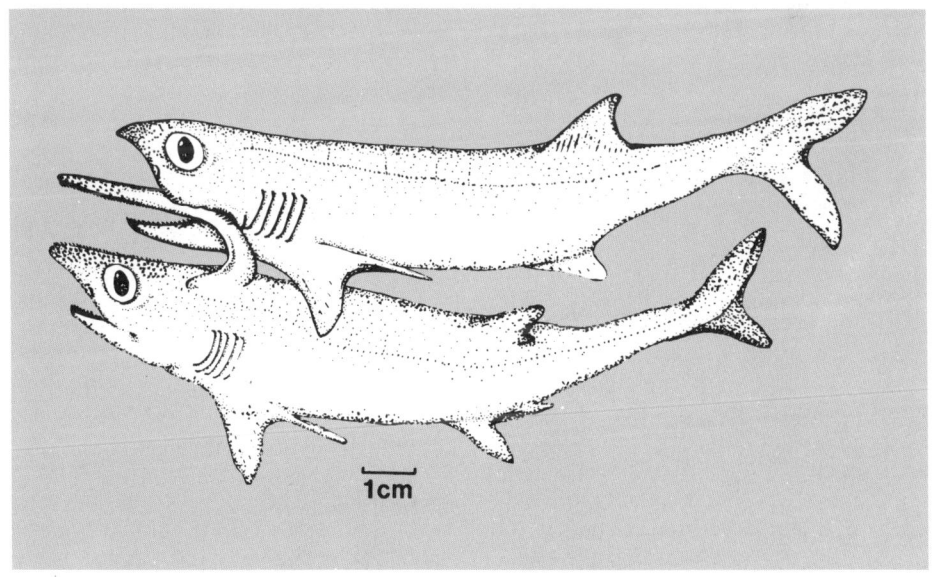

Male (below) and female (above) unicorn sharks, Falcatus falcatus, restored as displayed in the original fossils from the Bear Gulch Limestones.

A young Squatinactis montanus, from the Bear Gulch Limestones. Extended pectoral fins and spine near the tail are reminiscent of today's skates and rays. Specimen is only 3.1 inches (8 cm) across from tip to tip of the pectoral fins. Photo by R. Lund.

bore energetically extravagant ornamentation indicating that the evolutionary pressures in these species were directed toward attracting suitable mates, even at the price of swimming efficiency. Equally remarkable in these, and other Bear Gulch sharks, are several critical features that govern the lives of the cartilaginous fish today as well.

Reproductive strategies in modern sharks and their relatives center around internal fertilization, but more critically they center around a maximum investment of energy (nutrition) provided to a minimum number of offspring. Thus, sharks both now and back then have few young compared to bony fish, but these young are born relatively large, and well able to fend for themselves. This concentration on survival of rather few individuals contrasts strongly with the alternative strategy used by most bony fish, that of relying on high numbers of small offspring to insure the survival of some parental genes.

The shark-like fishes of today are equipped with one of the most fascinating senses, an ampullary system, that detects very weak electrical and magnetic fields. This system not only permits sharks to detect prey by the emanation of electrical fields from their bodies, but to navigate by the earth's magnetic field. There were a variety of sharks from the Bear Gulch Bay that obviously had fully elaborated ampullary systems, and thus were equipped with all the sensory modalities that render today's sharks such effective predators.

Finally, we get an answer of sorts to the old question of the origin of the chimaeras. Observations show that over 50% of the Bear Gulch shark species have specialized anatomical features more in common with today's chimaeras than with today's sharks, skates, and rays.

Bear Gulch was however only a moment in time. Many fossil deposits from the later Carboniferous follow some of the early lineages, while others disappear. Several forms of sharks populated fresh water, and among their fossils are some with anatomical, features closer to times yet to come. Spectacular and peculiar fragments of the fossil record exist, like arched and spiralled whorls of very large, serrated-edged teeth that fit between the junction of the lower jaws. Fragments and occasional specimens of those fish closer to the chimaeras recur infrequently. At the same time on land, obscure and agile species of four-footed animals apparently capable of laying eggs on dry land slowly gave rise to more, and more diverse lines of reptilian descendants.

The end of the Carboniferous, around 240 million years ago, saw the start of an environmental crisis across the Earth. The magnitude of this crisis was staggering, as glaciers, then worldwide deserts, then continental rifting, tore up all the old ecological relationships and exterminated a large percent of living species. Millions of years later, as climatic conditions settled down again, a completely new set of game strategies faced the survivors. The land-living reptiles had adapted so well that they were able to diversify and dominate land, sea, and air. Bony fishes altered drastically. Most of the old lineages of sharks slowly disappeared, leaving only a few odd experiments in how to build a chimaera. The shark record is almost non-existent, except of course for a few tantalizing forms with anatomical ties to times to come. These times arrived with the later dinosaurs, about 100 million years after the end of the Carboniferous. Our inability to adequately fill in this huge time gap is frustrating in the extreme.

What is known starts at the time of the first birds with fossil evidence of very few whole, small sharks. Then a jump over another time gap to the epochs when seas

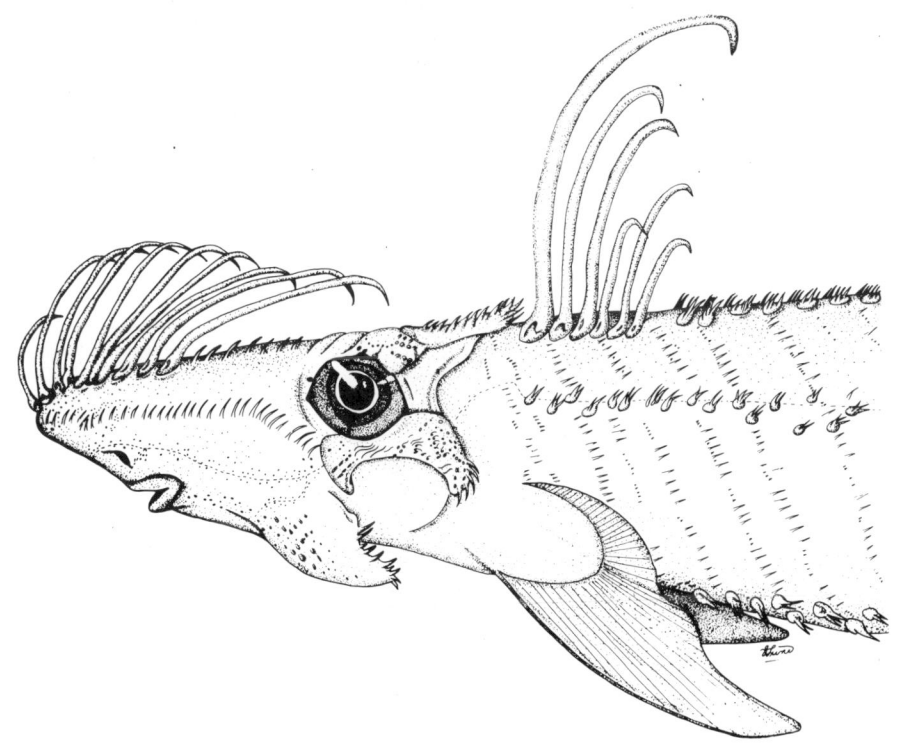

Reconstruction of unnamed distant relative of today's chimaeras shows paired sets of enlarged, hook-like scales that apparently adorned the head and forward dorsal section of the males. Original extended 3.6 inches (9 cm) from snout to base of pelvic fins.

deposited thick sequences of chalk across several continents. Somewhere around 100 million years ago, the teeth of sharks and skate-related forms resembling modern species, and occasionally entire jaws, start to be numerous in marine sediments. Teeth of recognizable mammals start to occur in terrestrial sediments. The large and varied contingent of seagoing reptiles continued to flourish and evolve, but for the first time they seemed to have competition. The details of the evolution of modern sharks are as yet unknown, lost in a wealth of little trays full of isolated teeth that may or may not differ in details from the isolated teeth of today's sharks, skates, and rays. With the rather sudden and well-publicized extinction of the dinosaurs around 65 million years ago, sharks were left to compete only with the bony fish, and once again, the evolutionary rules seem to have changed. The cartilaginous fish were now established in three rather specialized sets of conditions: sharks, skates and rays, and chimaeras. The bony fish diversified into many of the body forms and habitats we saw being occupied by sharks in the Carboniferous. Thus, from Italy and from Wyoming in the Eocene, (about 50 million years ago), stunningly beautiful fossil skate and ray-related fish glow like gems from their beds of rock. These were essentially modern forms, except for details. Elsewhere in the world, an evolutionary pattern was repeated as several groups of early mammals started the long process of adaptation to marine life.

Thus, diversification of the teleostean bony fish, and the whales, seals, dugongs, and other marine mammals, proceeded. With the evolution of these varied, but very efficient food sources, only the teeth and jaws are left to mark the evolution of the modern groups of sharks, skates, and rays. We can only speculate that the sensory, behavioral, and physiological evolution taking place within the constraints of the simple, efficient body designs that mark the sharks, skates and rays, and chimaeras, are the culmination of over 400 million years of changing evolutionary pressures and responses.

One thing is certain however; there is nothing "primitive" about today's sharks.

Thresher shark. Drawing by M. Levine

SHARK EARLY LIFE HISTORY:
One Reason Sharks Are Vulnerable to Overfishing

by STEVE BRANSTETTER

In the past, biologists often studied sharks to learn how to best protect man from sharks, but now research more commonly centers on how to best protect sharks from man. There has been such a rapid expansion in recreational and commercial shark fishing, that we may be catching sharks faster than they can reproduce themselves and sustain their population sizes.

Sharks are susceptible to intense fishing pressure. It is important that fishery managers know as much as possible about the sharks to utilize the resource efficiently. In the past few years biologists have learned a great deal about the life history of many shark species.

There are numerous interrelated components to a life history strategy, with several options available within each component. The different species place varying emphasis on the different options available. They each use slightly different methods to achieve the same end result — the successful reproduction of the species. Many sharks evolved a reproductive strategy that is more similar to mammals than other fishes. Instead of laying large numbers of eggs like most fishes, many sharks carry their young internally. During development these young derive their nourishment from the mother through a placental attachment, analogous to mammals. Thus there is limited space available for the development of the young. A mother can produce either several small young, or a few large young. However, once born, young sharks are on their own, receiving no parental care.

It is a fact of life that most young animals do not survive to adulthood. They may encounter unfavorable environmental conditions or fall prey to predators. Predatory risk to young sharks may be greatest from other sharks. Small sharks, either young sharks or adults of small species, are frequently eaten by large sharks. To avoid being eaten, it is necessary for them to grow to a size that will either: 1) deter predators from attacking, or 2) increase their swimming efficiency and speed so that they can actively avoid predation. Nursery grounds for the young reduce the predatory risk for many species. These nursery grounds can be categorized by the degree of exposure to potential predators. Some are "protected" by being located in areas infrequently inhabited by adult sharks. Others, in habitats occupied by adults, are "unprotected."

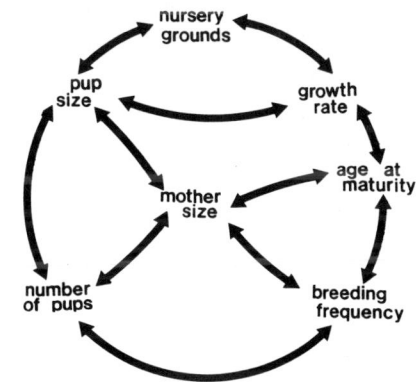

Generalized inter-relationship of various life history characteristics of viviparous sharks (after Branstetter 1990, NOAA Tech. Rep. NMFS 90).

A research scientist with the Virginia Institute of Marine Science, College of William and Mary, Gloucester Point, VA, Branstetter has studied the biology of sharks since 1977 and is examining the effects of fishing on shark stocks.

Although not true in all cases, the species that use protected nursery areas are very slow growing, and the young of species that occupy areas exposed to predators grow faster. In addition, small species which may suffer higher predation due to their size reach maturity more rapidly and reproduce more often than larger species.

Basically, shark species can be categorized as slow growing or fast growing. Within each of these categories, three sub-divisions are possible: 1) the production of a few large young; 2) the production of a few medium sized young; and 3) the production of numerous small young. The size and/or growth rate of the young is correlated to the type of nursery ground they use. Examples of each are outlined below. Sizes and growth will be discussed as comparisons of lengths, but it must be remembered that with increasing length also comes a cubic increase in girth and weight. For example a one-foot shark will weigh about a half-pound; a two-foot shark, five pounds; a three-foot shark, 10 pounds; a four-foot shark, 20 + pounds. Thus, increases in overall size, not just length, add to the possibility that the young sharks can deter predators.

Species with Slow Growth

LARGE YOUNG — Two coastal species, the sand tiger and the dusky shark, are common, large (10 feet) sharks that give birth to three-foot long pups. These pups spend their early life in shallow, beach front areas where they are exposed to predation by the adult sharks that also use this area. Dusky shark pups are often recorded as food items of adult sharks. Although they grow only about six inches in the first year, their large size may help them avoid predators.

Offshore species such as the white shark and longfin mako give birth to even larger pups, about four feet in length. These pups remain in offshore waters exposed to predators, but their large size may be sufficient to deter all except the largest predatory sharks.

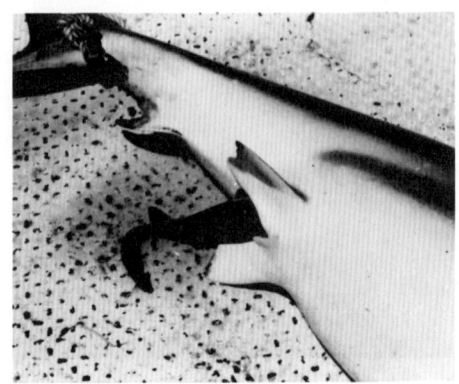

A. Spinner shark giving birth on deck.

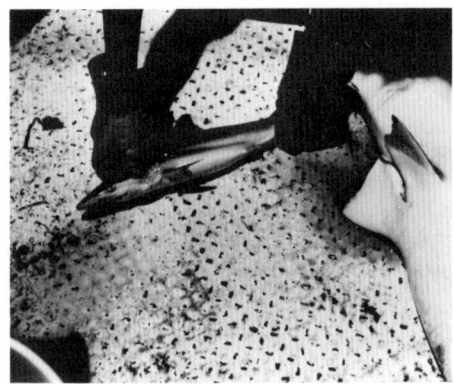

B. Two-foot long, fully developed Spinner shark pup.

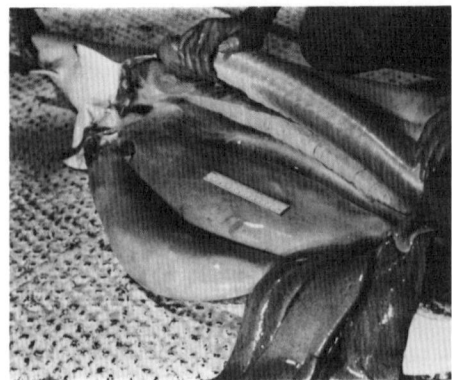

*C. Spinner shark body cavity showing remaining five pups of the litter. This species produces a few medium-sized young.
Photos by S. Branstetter.*

MEDIUM SIZED YOUNG — Slow growing species that produce medium-sized young have nursery grounds in protected areas such as bays, sounds, estuaries, or shallow reef flats that are not frequented by adult sharks. This group includes the bull, sandbar, and lemon sharks; all of which give birth to pups about two feet long. At this size they are much more susceptible to predation than the larger pups mentioned above. In fact, adult bull sharks are known to commonly prey on juvenile sandbar sharks. These sharks also grow only about six inches during their first year; thus they have a better chance for survival if they remain in areas where adults do not occur. Major nurseries for the bull shark are the estuarine areas of the northern Gulf of Mexico. Chesapeake Bay is a major nursery for the sandbar shark, and the shallow flats of the Florida Keys are often used by juvenile lemon sharks. Even when they are in these "protected" nurseries, first year mortality rates of 50% may occur.

The pups of all three species frequent the nurseries for several years. Juveniles of a size corresponding to one year old sharks are common in the nurseries. After two to three years when the juveniles have attained lengths of four feet, they move out to continental shelf waters and begin living with the larger, older shark populations.

SMALL YOUNG — Another slow growing species, the scalloped hammerhead, uses the third strategy: production of more numerous small young. As adults these 10-foot sharks occupy offshore waters. They come inshore to give birth to as many as 30 young that are only about 1.5 feet long. The pups live in bays and sounds for about six months, then they move out to beach and coast waters where they are exposed to predators. Young-of-the-year scalloped hammerheads are often recorded as food of other sharks. This apparent high mortality may be offset by the larger number of young produced.

In all these instances however, slow growth has its limitations — a relatively long period of vulnerability, so the pups must avoid areas inhabited by the adults.

Species with Fast Growth

In contrast, a number of species have much faster growth rates. Their pups may occupy definite nursery grounds, but the nurseries are not as "protected" as those of the slow growing species and are usually restricted to high salinity areas such as shallow water beach fronts frequented by adult sharks. This category includes coastal and offshore species, and species that reach a maximum size of only three feet to those that exceed lengths of 10 feet.

Extremes in this group are the small species, including the sharpnose, bonnethead, smalltail, finetooth, and blacknose sharks. These species reach maximum sizes of three to five feet, and produce very small pups compared to most species. Their small size, even as adults, makes them susceptible to predation throughout life.

Mechanisms have evolved in the life histories of these species to counterbalance the increased chance of mortality. Where many of the larger species have a one-year resting stage between pregnancies, many of the small species do not. The bonnethead gestation period is only about four to five months. The Atlantic sharpnose shark has an 11-month gestation period, and rebreeds approximately one month after giving birth. The sharpnose matures in three to four years, in contrast to the slow growing species that take 15 years to mature. The females produce 4-6 young per litter which are as large as can be accommodated in their body cavities. A three-foot female gives birth to pups that are about 13 inches long. At this size the pups are very vulnerable to predators and occupy protected nurseries. They grow rapidly and are two feet long in a year's time, but this is still smaller than many newborn pups of other species. The rapid growth rate, early maturation, and short

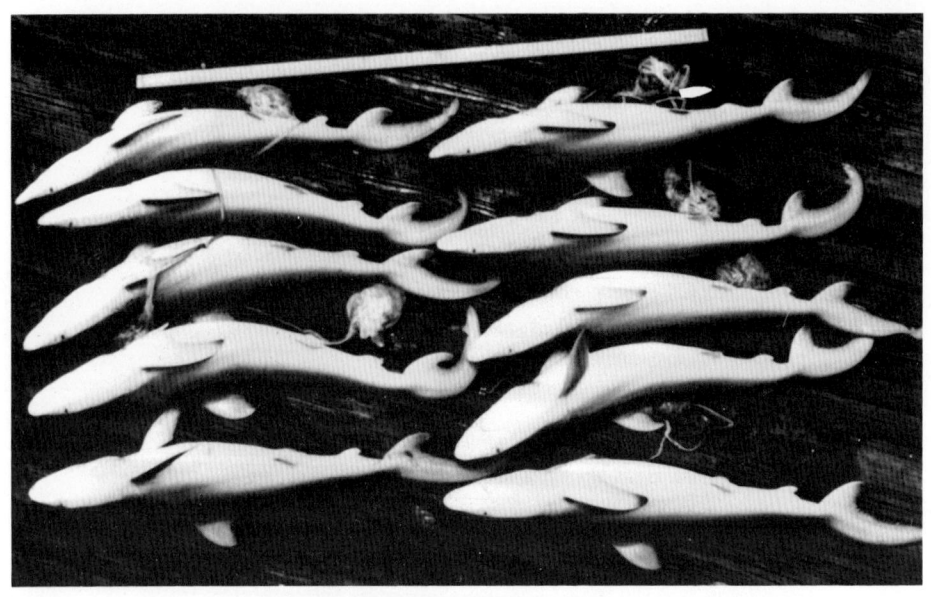
Fully developed dusky shark litter. Each pup is about three feet long. Photo by S. Branstetter.

reproductive cycles are all indicative of a higher mortality on these small shark species.

LARGE YOUNG — Some fast growing species produce large young. The thresher sharks produce 2-4 pups that are two to three feet long, excluding the exaggerated upper caudal fin. The pups grow quickly, increasing about a foot a year in length. The long upper caudal fin may be of further help in deterring predators by giving the impression that the pups are much larger.

MEDIUM SIZED YOUNG — Larger coastal sharks, such as the spinner and blacktip sharks, also grow rapidly as newborns. These pups, two feet long at birth, occupy beach front areas their first summer, and are exposed to predators. They increase to 3-4 feet in a year's time and continue to grow 6-8 inches per year for the next couple of years.

Some open ocean sharks have similar life histories although the young do not use coastal nurseries. The silky shark, a large 10-foot shark of the outer continental shelf, gives birth to pups about two feet long. These pups use deep-water reef areas as early nurseries, but move to a pelagic existence by six months of age. They stay in schools segregated from the adults, growing to 3-4 feet by one year of age. Similarly, the shortfin mako produces 6-18 young about two feet in length that remain in offshore waters. These sharks grow even faster than a foot a year. This coupled with their swimming speed reduces predation pressure.

SMALL YOUNG — Blue sharks and tiger sharks also have rapid growth rates, but they produce comparatively large numbers of young suggesting that mortality rates on the young may be higher than for other species. They both give birth to numerous (40-80) comparatively small young. Newborn blue shark pups are only about 1.5 feet long and stay in epipelagic oceanic waters where they are vulnerable to predation. The pups nearly double in length their first year and continue rapid growth for the next two or three years. Even so, mortality may be high on these young sharks considering the number produced by each female. The tiger shark gives birth to 40-70 two-foot-long young pups that are very slender and swim in an eel-like fashion,

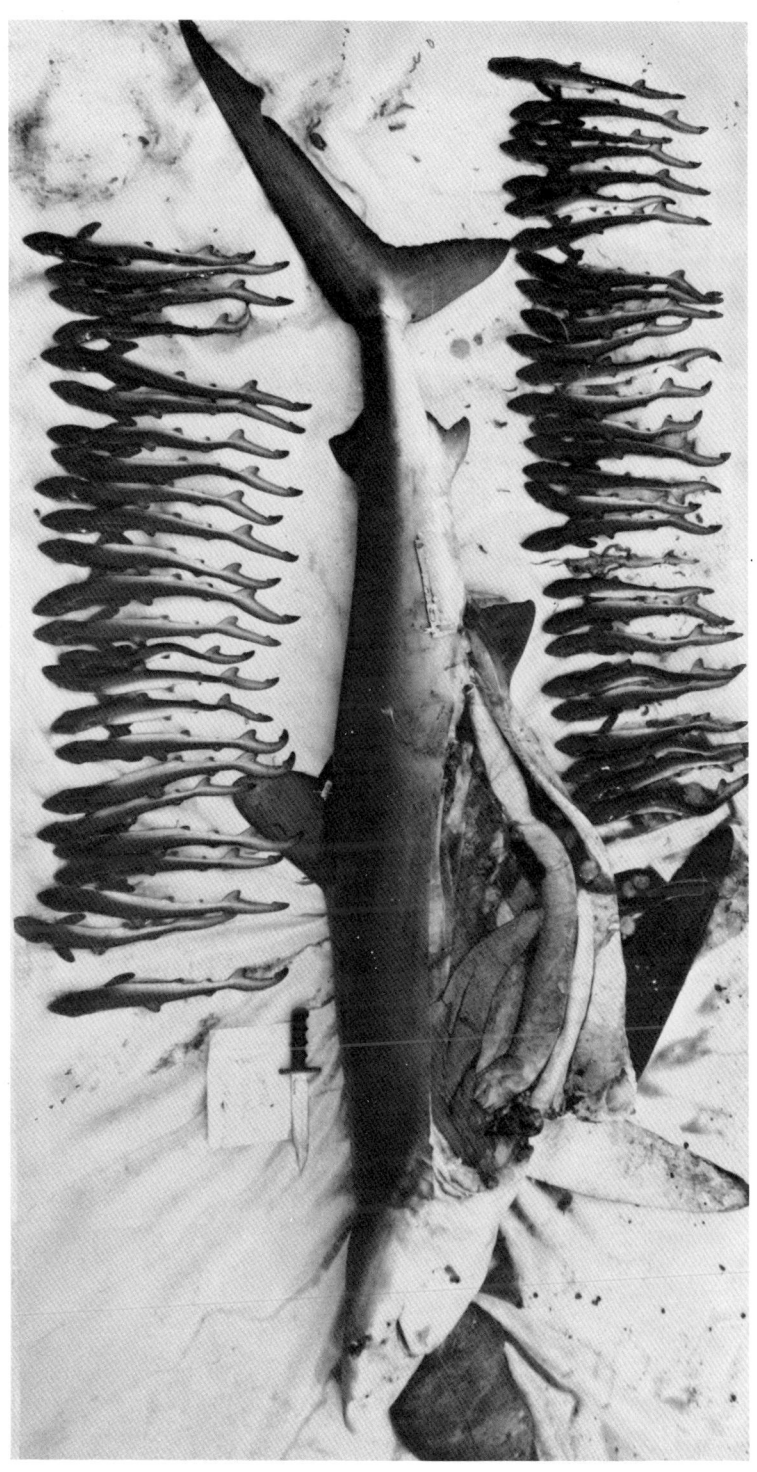
Blue shark with litter of 51 pups, each about 1.5 feet long. Photo by H.W. Pratt.

precluding rapid swimming speeds. They grow rapidly, doubling in length the first year of life. Rapid linear growth continues for the next two years until the lengths exceed six feet.

In conclusion, we find that different shark species emphasize different life history characteristics for adequate reproductive success. Attaining lengths of three feet may be critical for newborn survival as the pups are then large enough to deter many predators as well as actively avoid predation through increased swimming speed and efficiency. This may be accomplished by two strategies: 1) rapid growth in nursery grounds exposed to predators, or 2) slow growth in protected nursery grounds. Those small species which are nearing their maximum size at three feet are probably susceptible to predation throughout their life history, but offset this higher mortality rate with more numerous offspring produced.

Biologists still do not know enough about specific life history details of many shark species, such as age-specific mortality. It can however be assumed that juveniles of each species suffer high mortality. The increasing exploitation of adult stocks may result in reduced future reproduction, leading to insufficient recruitment, and eventual collapse of populations. Because of the multispecies nature of the developing shark fishery, management at the group level is desirable, but difficult to achieve due to the variations in the life history strategies employed by the different species.

Pregnant lemon shark.
Photo by R. Jureit.

Anatomical Features of Sharks and Their Allies

by SANFORD MOSS

Most people believe they are looking at a shark when they see a fish that has several gill slits, an underslung jaw, a caudal fin with a large upper lobe, and skin that feels like sandpaper. Indeed, these well known characters are borne by many, if not most, true sharks, but certainly not all elasmobranchs. Sharks are anatomically distinct, but their obvious characteristics often reflect more telling features that are hidden from all but the most enquiring eyes. Moreover, there are myriad fine details in the construction of sharks, skates, and rays that warrant our attention if we are to fully appreciate these marvelous fishes.

In the space permitted we will look at familiar shark features as well as some aspects of the brain, skeleton, and muscular systems that are less well known. Other articles in this issue that deal with sensory, feeding, and reproductive systems of sharks provide more examples of anatomical specializations. These glimpses into the living shark should help us understand that sharks are highly adapted, specialized animals more worthy of our admiration than disdain.

All elasmobranch fishes have several separate gill slits through which respiratory water passes from the animal's pharynx to the outside. Blood coursing through the gill filaments exchanges carbon dioxide for vital oxygen. Gills also participate in salt regulation and may have other functions as well. Sharks have from five to seven slits, depending upon the species. In many of them the first gill slit is modified as a "spiracle," an opening between the hyoid (a modified gill arch that helps support the jaws) and the first normal gill arch. The spiracle is most noticeable in skates and rays, where it is the only gill slit found on the upper surface of these flattened animals. It is also well developed in the dogfishes but is reduced or even missing in many others, including the requiem, hammerhead, and mackerel sharks.

Among the skates and rays the spiracle functions as an inhalant opening through which water passes into the pharynx while the fish is lying partially buried in bottom sediments. In embryonic rays it also provides a route for delivery of nourishing uterine secretions to the digestive tract. Spiracles in dogfishes and other sharks seem to serve less of a breathing function than a sensory one since these spiracles are equipped with special organs well supplied with nerves.

Shark gill filaments receive unique backing from the connective tissue plates to which they are bonded. Each plate extends from a cartilaginous gill bar that supports it on the pharyngeal side to the exterior where the plate ends at the skin. The plates work to keep the respiratory water streams separate throughout their passage from pharynx to outside.

Although we need to learn more about how sharks pump water over their gills, multiple gill slits seem to limit the way water is moved. Bony fishes, with a single external opercular opening, use the operculum to suck water across the gills, even as more water is being drawn into the mouth. Water flow over the gills of these fishes is more continuous than pulsing. Sharks, however, use only a pressure pump method that squeezes water across the gills as the mouth and pharyngeal cavities are contracted. While most fish

---

Moss is a professor of biology at Southeastern Massachusetts University, North Dartmouth, where he conducts research on functional morphology and behavior of elasmobranchs and chemical communication among teleosts. He wrote Natural History of the Antarctic Peninsula, *Columbia University Press, 1988.*

can irrigate their gills by simply opening their mouths when swimming rapidly (ram ventilation), sharks switch to this mode at slower swimming speeds. Although it is commonly thought that sharks must swim to breathe, in fact many sharks frequently rest on the bottom and are perfectly able to irrigate their gills by pharyngeal pumping. Only oceanic sharks rely completely on ram ventilation for if they remained motionless for a period, they would sink toward the abyss.

The importance of ram ventilation in sharks helps to explain the purpose of multiple gill slits. By having separate gill covers and muscular control over their constriction, fine adjustments can be made in the resistance to water movement through the various gill openings. This allows for continual adjustments of flow across the various gills, maintaining optimum respiratory performance.

Most sharks and rays have ventral mouths. "Chinless cowards" is how diving pioneer and naturalist William Beebe described sharks. While the underslung jaw is characteristic, it is not diagnostic. Many ancestral sharks had mouths extending to the tips of their snouts, as do a few modern ones (frill, megamouth, angel sharks and devil rays). Rather than being a primitive, or even a cumbersome element of shark anatomy, the ventral mouth is a highly adapted feature that helps sharks achieve their ecological status as apex ocean predators.

An advantage of the underslung jaw is that it allows room for anchoring massive jaw muscles that cannot be housed by fishes with mouths opening at the tips of their snouts. Shark jaw muscles are positioned to create large biting forces transmitted through short jaws, and to allow independent movement of these jaws with respect to the rest of the head. The resulting feeding apparatus lets a shark carve chunks of flesh out of prey too large to be taken at a bite. Rare among fishes, this ability evolved in the Mesozoic Era and signalled the end of the evolutionary fish strategy of using large body size to escape predation.

The common belief that a mouth on the belly side is awkward is belied by the success of elasmobranchs. Most of these fishes find their food on the ocean floor where it is easily sucked into the ventral mouth. The mobility of both the upper and lower jaws allows them to pick up objects in midwater, as well as to cut deeply into large prey. The sensory information that guides sharks during the final stages of a feeding attack is electrical in nature. Their mouths lie at the geometric centers of arrays of ampullary pores that lead the shark to food just as unerringly as we "look" forks full of food into our own mouths. Rather than being a clumsy impediment to feeding, the ventral mouth is an anatomical feature that appeared relatively recently in shark evolution and provides an elegant way to handle food.

Many sharks have a distinctive caudal fin with the upper lobe larger than the lower. This "heterocercal" tail is not unique to sharks since bony fishes like sturgeons and paddle fishes have it too, but it is a consistent feature of most familiar sharks. The importance of this form of tail can be appreciated by looking at the sharks, skates, and rays that lack it. Sluggish and bottom-oriented sharks like wobbegongs, some catsharks, and most benthic skates and rays, have tail fins that are either nearly symmetrical (electric rays), reduced or absent altogether (stingrays, devil rays, eagle rays, many skates), have an expanded lower lobe (angel sharks), or the lower lobe is so reduced that the upper one functions as practically the entire tail fin (wobbegongs, nurse sharks, catsharks). The heterocercal tail is restricted to sharks that are accomplished swimmers and are active in the water column for a fair percentage of time.

The faster swimmers tend to have more erect tail fins, and an inclination to larger lower lobes, which in some cases (mackerel sharks) approach the upper

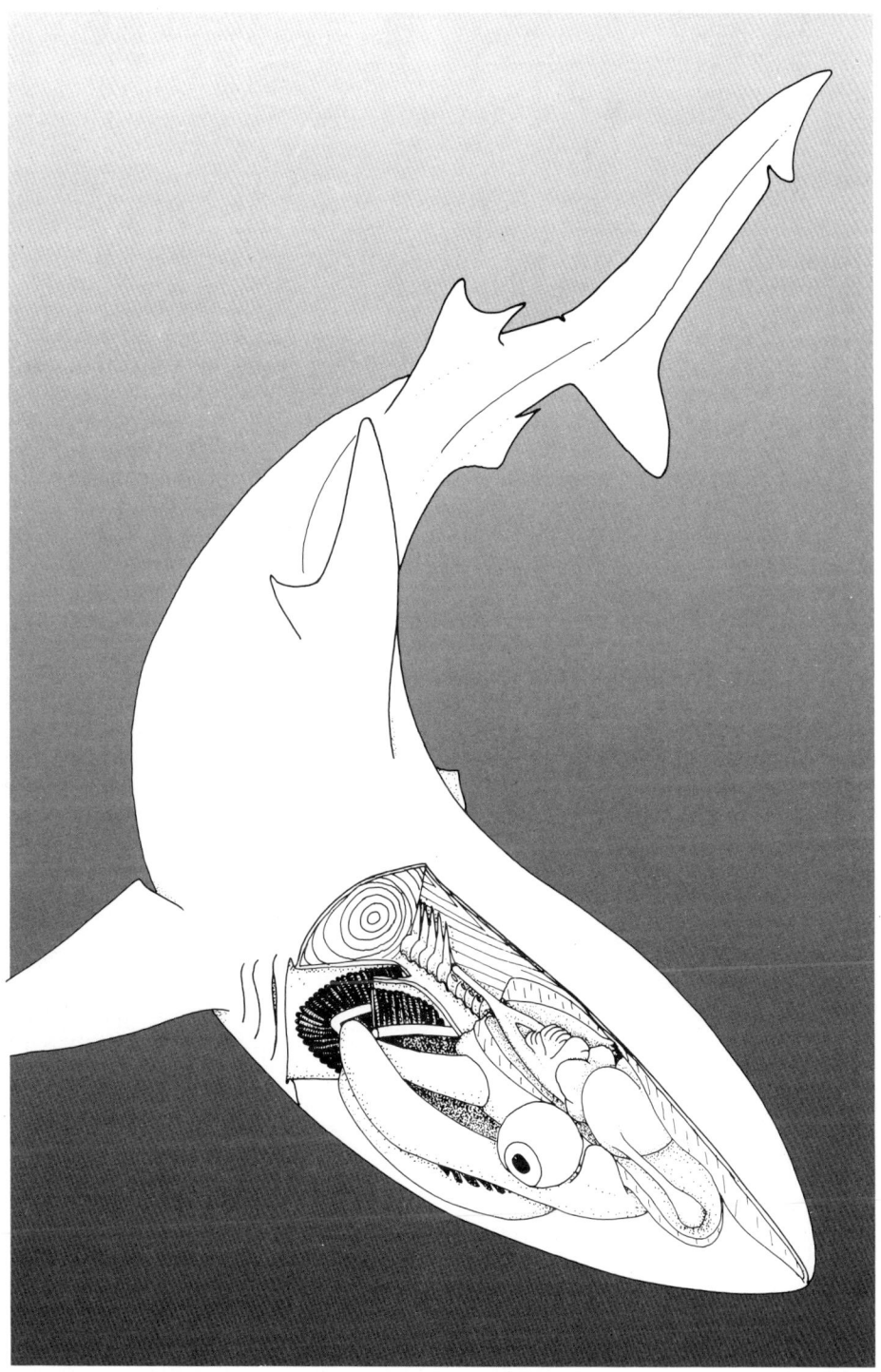

Simplified transparent view of typical requiem shark showing anatomical relationship of brain, braincase, jaws, hyomandibula, and gills. Drawing by S. Moss.

lobe in size. Among the slower sharks we find the best examples of the "typical" shark tail fin, including the requiem sharks, hammerheads, and sand tiger sharks. For a shark to swim well, it needs a heterocercal tail. For it to swim very well, the caudal fin approaches a symmetrical form.

A key to the distinctive shark tail fin form is that unlike most bony fishes, sharks, skates, and rays have no gas or air bladder to change their relative buoyancy. Instead sharks depend on their upper caudal lobes to develop thrust, and use their pectoral fins and other body surfaces as diving planes to adjust their position in the water column. The lower caudal lobe makes fine alterations in the thrust direction. Slow moving sharks that have pronounced lower caudal lobes (basking sharks and deep-sea dogfishes like cookie cutter sharks) usually have large, oil-rich livers that provide enough flotation to keep their position in the water column with little forward speed.

It may seem that the shark's failure to evolve a gas-filled bladder for buoyancy control is another indication of its lowliness. Lack of swim bladders is actually advantageous to sharks in that they are not captive to a narrow range of water depths. A large grouper cannot quickly move very far vertically without running the risk of collapsing its gas bladder and sinking like a stone, or ballooning to the surface as its bladder expands during rapid ascent. A shark, on the other hand, can move easily throughout a wide range of depths without suffering such restrictions. Large, fast-swimming bony fishes like tunas that sometimes forage at great depths have lost or greatly reduced their swim bladders.

The skin of many sharks (called "shagreen" when dried and used as sandpaper) owes its sandpaper-like character to firmly embedded placoid scales which are structurally quite different from the overlapping scales of most bony fish. Each is formed like a small tooth, complete with dentin base (embedded in the dermis), pulp cavity, dentin core, and an enamel surface to the protruding cusp. In some sharks like the bramble sharks, but especially in skates, individual placoid scales can be large and act as defensive spines, shields, and bucklers. But in sharks more adept at swimming, these scales take on additional roles. They are shaped more like mushrooms and have expanded rectangular or stellate bases with narrower necks and streamlined crowns projecting above them. The crowns have three to five longitudinal ridges and often an additional microscopic relief pattern of hexagonal or octagonal pockets. While individual

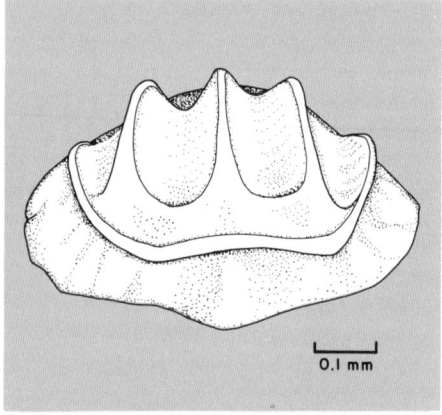

Typical placoid scale of requiem shark showing expanded base embedded in the skin and longitudinal ridges that decrease drag. Drawing by S. Moss

scales get larger as a shark grows (probably through replacement and the addition of new scales), the maximum size for most of the faster swimming sharks peaks out at about 0.6 mm (.02 inches) wide by about 0.5 mm (.019 inches) long. The height of the ridges and their separation remain fairly constant in most species. The scales are arranged so that the ridges run parallel to the direction water flows over the shark's body. Similar patterns of grooves or striations on boat hulls and aircraft have improved performance by significantly reducing drag. Placoid scales, often considered further examples of the "primitive" nature of sharks, are really superb adaptations that allow sharks to slip through water with an efficiency unmatched by most other organisms.

Additional anatomical refinements, found deeper in the bodies of sharks, further demonstrate a high degree of adaptation. Consider the following examples:

SKELETON — A shark's skeleton is made mostly of cartilage (some sharks do have small amounts of true bone) that can be strengthened by deposits of minerals (apatite) in areas subjected to special stress such as the jaws and vertebrae. While cartilage is often considered an embryonic tissue (and therefore primordial), it is an ideal tissue for sharks. Cartilage is lighter than bone (important for animals without gas bladders); it is flexible (most sharks are exceedingly supple and can virtually turn on a dime); and it can grow throughout the life of a shark.

BRAIN — Sharks have traditionally been considered dim intellects, yet many of them have brain sizes that are relatively enormous when compared to other fishes. The shark's ratio of brain to body weight puts many of them in the same ball park as some birds (ostriches) and mammals (some marsupials). Requiem and mackerel sharks have large forebrains and complex cerebellums; eagle and stingrays have the most complex brains. We don't completely understand the meaning of large brains in these fishes, but in sharks it could reflect both the great sensory capabilities as well as the coordinated manner of swimming.

ELECTRIC ORGANS — Some elasmobranchs have special electrogenic organs. The electric rays (torpedoes) have large, compact electric organs derived from muscle cells associated with the pectoral fins. With coin-like stacks of cells acting like tiny batteries, wired both in series and in parallel, these rays produce electric currents in brief pulses that are strong enough (as high as 200

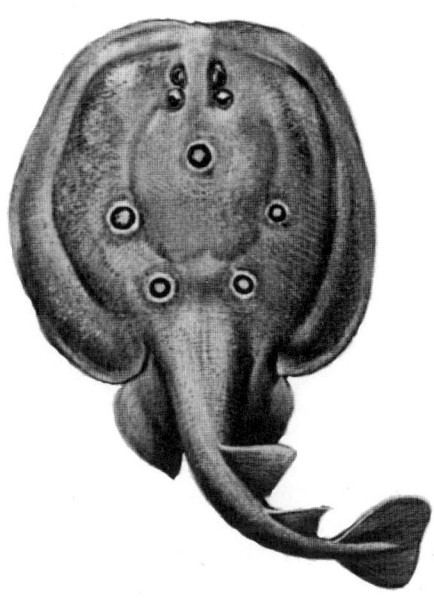

Torpedo.

volts with up to 50 amperes) to immobilize their fish prey.

Skates also have electric organs. Although they too use modified muscles to produce electric discharges, the position and functions of their organs are much different from those of the torpedoes. Instead skates have narrow bands of tissue running down both sides of their tails which discharge only about one volt of electricity. The function of these electric organs is still debated, but may have to do with social communication, food location, or defense.

RETE MIRABILE — One of the more spectacular shark adaptations involves the circulatory system of lamniform sharks like makos, whites, and threshers which have special regions of juxtaposed arterioles and small veins that allow them to recycle their body heat, minimizing its loss to the outside. The temperature of the trunk muscles and viscera can be held at levels well above that of the environment, which increases the speed and power of muscle contraction, the rate of digestion, and the development of embryos. Special organs, called retia mirabilia, pass oxygen-rich, cool arterial blood coming from the gills, close to warm venous blood returning from the interior of the shark. Heat from the venous blood moves across the thin blood vessel walls to the cooler arterial blood in what amount to counter-current heat exchangers, effectively keeping that heat from being lost. The retia mirabilia are found in two places. The blood draining the vast bulk of the trunk musculature passes through retia near the lateral surface of the body, while blood draining from the visceral organs gives up its heat to arteries bringing blood from greatly enlarged pericardial arteries. The result is that these sharks are able to control their body temperatures, effectively making them "warm-blooded."

This brief overview of some features of shark anatomy can hardly do justice to the structural elegance of these animals. With each new investigation we better understand that the stereotypical picture of sharks as archaic, blood-thirsty behemoths has impeded our appreciation of them. Watching them soar gracefully through their watery world, we can more easily appreciate that they are as perfectly tuned to their environment as the gulls that soar through the air above them.

ADDITIONAL READING:

Moss, S.A. 1984. Sharks. A GUIDE FOR THE AMATEUR NATURALIST. Prentice-Hall (Englewood Cliffs, N.J.).

Springer, V.G. and J.P. Gold. 1989. SHARKS IN QUESTION. Smithsonian Institution Press (Washington, D.C.).

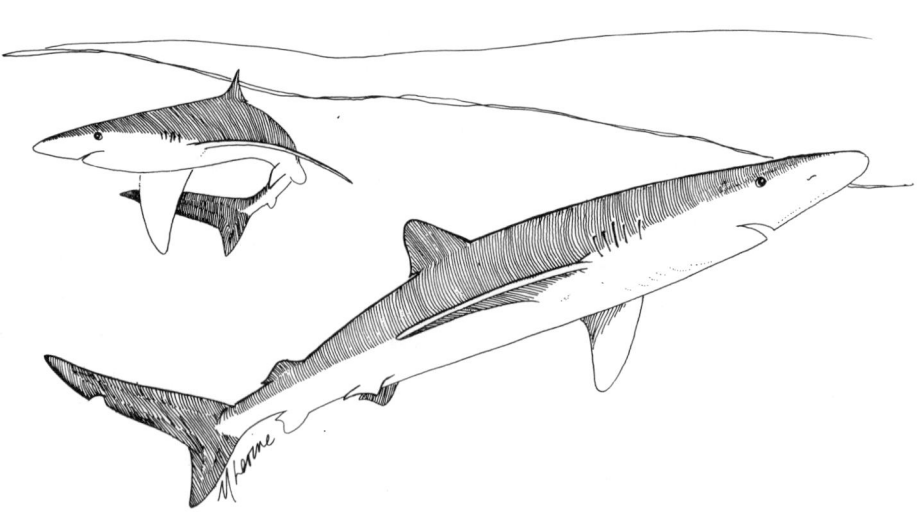

Blue shark. Drawing by M. Levine

The Unique Roles of Two Liver Products In Suiting Sharks to their Environment

by THOMAS B. THORSON

The liver is an organ found in all vertebrate animals. It is a sophisticated chemical factory which produces, stores, secretes, or in some way processes or even destroys a great variety of substances that play important parts in the normal functioning of the vertebrate's body. Prominent among the internal organs of all vertebrate groups, the liver is especially large among the cartilaginous fishes. It usually comprises from 20 to 30 percent of total body weight but, depending to varying degrees on size (age), sex, food supply, season of year, reproductive condition, etc., the percentage may substantially exceed or fall short of this range.

There is a basic likeness in vertebrate livers and their functions. They all deal with a variety of syntheses, transformations, and disposition of the metabolized end products of all three major food types: carbohydrates, fats, and proteins. It would be impossible to deal with all of these functions, even briefly, in this short article. There are, however, certain features of elasmobranch liver function that are so nearly unique to this group of fishes and so important in their adaptation to their environmental needs that I have selected just two of them for discussion.

Some sharks produce high percentages of oils (fats or lipids) in relatively large livers, making them both unique and remarkable. Sharks have few natural predators, but these liver oils have attracted the attention of the supreme predators (humankind) in their search for natural animal products with trade value. The oils have been sold for use as fixatives in perfume manufacture, as a base for certain paints, in the production of various cosmetic products, as lubricants for fine machinery, and as folk remedies for any number of ills. Liver oils also have a number of applications in modern medicine. During the 1940's a number of shark populations were heavily exploited for the high content of Vitamin A in their livers. Since then Vitamin A has been produced synthetically.

Biologists were more interested in discovering the explanation for the copious oil supply, which may sometimes reach as much as 80 or even 90 percent of the liver weight. The easiest and most logical explanation was that the stored oil provides a supply of energy which can be drawn upon when food supply is short, or the sharks are not feeding for any other reason. This was, in fact, regarded as *the* explanation until the past decade or two. Now it is apparent that, although the oil may be drawn on for energy under certain circumstances, the sharks use the oil for another important function — by regulating the amount of certain oils stored in the liver, sharks adjust the overall density of their bodies. In other words, the oils are used to regulate the body's buoyancy.

An organism that is heavier than the water surrounding it has negative buoyancy and will tend to sink; if lighter than the water it has positive buoyancy and will tend to rise to the surface. In either case, energy must be expended to move up or down in the water column opposite the gravitational tendency. If the organism has neutral buoyancy, no

Thorson is professor emeritus of zoology at the University of Nebraska, Lincoln, where he also served as department chairman and vice director, School of Biological Sciences. Since 1961 his research has concentrated on freshwater adaptation in elasmobranchs with emphasis on the bull shark and sawfish of Lake Nicaragua and the stingrays of the rivers of South America and Nigeria.

energy is expended to maintain its vertical position and very little to make a moderate change in depth. Cartilaginous skeletons help sharks reduce their weight in water but are no help in the short-term regulation of buoyancy — a function performed by the gas bladder in bony fishes. This is where the liver oils come into the picture.

Shark liver oil is a blend of many fats and fat-like substances which are of relatively low density, have a specific gravity of less than 1.0 (the specific gravity of distilled water under a set of standard conditions), and are produced in various proportions in different species of sharks. Most noteworthy and probably best known of the oils is *squalene*, which is characterized by chemists as an unsaturated hydrocarbon with a chemical formula of $C_{30}H_{50}$ and a specific gravity of 0.86. Most other liver oils have specific gravities of 0.900 - 0.925 among pelagic shark species, and 0.926 - 0.940 in bottom-dwelling species. The specific gravity of various shark tissues, muscle, skin, cartilage, etc., (not including the livers) is somewhat greater than that of water (about 1.06 - 1.09), but the mixed densities of these and the lighter liver oils, often mostly squalene, bring the density of the whole shark to a level only slightly heavier than that of water (most fresh water has a specific gravity near 1.000; average seawater 1.026).

In order to avoid sinking to the bottom, many sharks must be in constant movement. The pectoral fins supply most of the lift to counteract gravitational pull, and the caudal fin (tail) provides most of the forward thrust. In these sharks, the energy required for constant, day and night movement can be provided by the shark's metabolism if the movement is made at a leisurely pace. With the sharply increased energy expenditure required in a burst of speed, such as during pursuit of fast-moving prey, or escaping an enemy, the shark can continue for only a limited time before exhaustion forces it out of the race. A somewhat similar situation can be demonstrated experimentally, by producing a change in density of the shark's body. If the specific gravity is increased, either by attaching weights to its body or by bleeding off some of its low density liver oils, the tendency to sink increases sharply and a great deal more vigorous swimming is required to prevent sinking. If the stress of the extra weight is not relieved, the shark will be exhausted and in spite of its exertion, will eventually find itself on the bottom. Conversely, if the shark's specific gravity is experimentally decreased, (perhaps by introducing air into its stomach or body cavity) and it reaches neutral buoyancy (specific gravity of the shark body and the environmental water are equal), the hydrodynamics of the shark's swimming movements would be so altered that its locomotor coordination, orientation, and maneuverability would break down, making it unable to swim normally or pursue prey successfully.

In normal daily or seasonal activities, situations no doubt arise when the specific gravity of the shark's body changes in relation to that of the water. Some of these changes might take place during seasonal air temperature fluctuations, causing cooling or heating of surface water and resulting in movements of sharks from inshore, shallow waters to deeper and denser offshore waters, or vice versa. Or changes can occur when sharks move along the coast and pass from water of high salinity (high density water) through brackish, or even fresh water around rivermouths, or vice versa. Other changes might also occur within the shark such as the quantity of oils produced, or in the mixture of various oils which have different specific gravities. These changes might stem from fluctuations in food consumption due either to scarcity of food or species specific feeding behaviors such as suspension of feeding by males during the breeding season and by females giving birth. In live-bearing species, especially those that nourish their young through a placenta after the yolks of their large eggs have been depleted, the female's food reserves (oils) may also be used.

It seems reasonable that, if the liver's stored energy were extensively tapped, the buoyancy-regulation function might be impaired, resulting in deteriorating swimming coordination and general effectiveness. However, this does not seem to be the case. The best evidence now indicates that, when the need for oils for the buoyancy-regulating function comes into competition with the need for oils as an energy reserve during prolonged food deprivation, the buoyancy control function takes priority.

We have very little knowledge on either the exact chemical or physical mechanisms that convey the need for buoyancy adjustment to the appropriate cells of the liver, and how these cells are stirred into action, or are inhibited from delivering their product. Whatever the reason may be for fluctuations in the ratio of densities between the shark and the environmental water, appropriate responses must be elicited or dire consequences may follow. However, well before those consequences might occur, the remarkable system evolved by the sharks for fine-tuning their body density kicks in. An adjustment is *automatically* made in the kinds and/or the blend of low and high density liver oils, and the sharks go on their way, swimming gracefully night and day, maintaining an appropriate depth in the water and optimum energy efficiency for swimming — all without the help of a gas bladder.

The second unique use of liver products in the cartilaginous fishes involves the excretory process.

The early steps of carbohydrate and fat processing take place in the digestive tract. Later metabolic stages take place in the liver. The final end products are water and carbon dioxide. If present in excess of any special needs, they are easily disposed of. Proteins, in addition to water and carbon dioxide, produce nitrogenous wastes which pose special problems in the excretion process. Nitrogen is the most characteristic element of proteins. A nitrogen atom is the central atom of each of the amino groups that make up the various amino acids, the building blocks which link up to produce

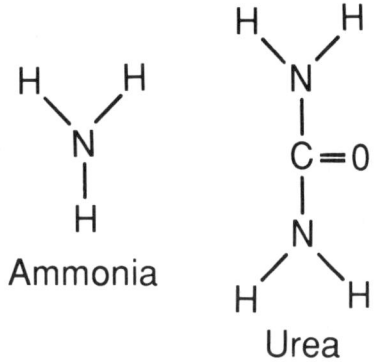

Structural formulas of ammonia and urea (C=carbon; O=oxygen; N=nitrogen; H=hydrogen).

the protein molecules. When these molecules are metabolized in the liver, the amino acids are split apart and then degraded to ammonia, NH_3, which is the basic, simplest nitrogenous waste produced in all vertebrates and most invertebrates. Ammonia is highly soluble and the most easily excreted nitrogenous waste. It is the main waste product of the bony fishes, and most of the amphibians and invertebrates. It passes out of the body through any soft tissue in direct contact with the environmental water, such as the body surface, the lining of the mouth, and the gills. In elevated quantities ammonia is highly toxic, so it can't be the main waste product in animals that are unable to excrete it directly into the water, and therefore have to store it for some time. Such is the case with mammals (including humans), and the more terrestrial of the amphibians, both of which convert their waste nitrogen largely to urea, a compound which combines two ammonia molecules with a carbon dioxide (CO_2) molecule. Urea is highly soluble, is non-toxic in ordinary concentrations, and its molecules carry twice the nitrogen carried by ammonia molecules.

The great amount of water required to dissolve and excrete nitrogen in the form of urea is intolerable for highly terrestrial vertebrates such as birds and reptiles, which need to conserve every drop of water possible. This is especially true in the developmental stages which take place in enclosed eggs where nitrogenous wastes must accumulate until hatching. In either the ammonia or urea form, concentrations within the egg would become highly toxic and kill the embryos long before hatching. This problem is solved by conversion (in the liver) of the nitrogen wastes into the nearly insoluble form of uric acid which carries four nitrogen atoms per uric acid molecule. It is stored in a white crystalline paste or liquid form seen easily in the fecal material of birds and is usually accompanied by very little water loss and virtually no toxicity.

Hypothetically, elasmobranchs might be expected to excrete nitrogen as ammonia, as do the bony fishes, but as their evolution has turned out, they convert the nitrogen to urea and are the most notorious producers of urea. Not only do they produce more urea than bony fishes, but instead of excreting it, their gill membranes and kidneys act as "urea dams" that retain the urea and build up high concentrations in the blood as well as in all the other body fluids. Such high concentrations would poison and kill bony fishes and humans. Elasmobranchs not only can tolerate them but actually use them to their own benefit as we shall see.

Besides urea, there are a number of other forms of nitrogenous end products produced in the elasmobranch liver. One of these is trimethylamine oxide (TMAO). These products are sometimes present in fairly large quantities and play the same role as urea in their effect on the osmotic concentration of body fluids, although they have other important functions as well.

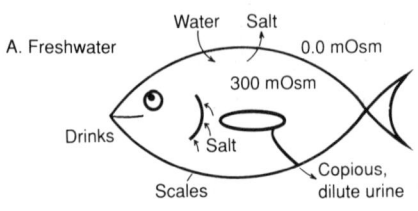

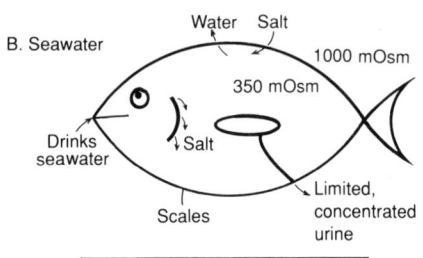

Osmoregulatory mechanisms of bony fishes (Osteichthyes).

In order to understand the unique and beneficial use of urea by elasmobranchs, as a means of regulating the osmotic concentration of their body fluids, we need first to look at how the bony fishes (the teleosts) maintain their internal water and salt concentrations at relatively constant levels. For example fluids (blood plasma, pericardial fluid, etc.) of a freshwater fish have salts and other substances (collectively called solutes) dissolved or otherwise suspended in them in certain concentration. Solute concentraions are expressed in various units of which we shall arbitrarily, and without technical definition, use the osmole. Osmotic concentrations in animal fluids usually fall in a range where milliosmoles (thousands of an osmole, abreviated as m0sm) are the appropriate unit to use. Here the fluids of freshwater bony fishes contain approximately 300 mMol of solutes, while the water outside the body (environmental water) contains almost no solutes. Its concentration is here represented as 0.0, although there is at least a trace of solute in all natural water. The water outside the body is separated from the solution inside by a biological membrane consisting of the skin, gills, mouth cavity, and other scaleless areas. Here we have a classic illustration of salt diffusion and osmotic passage of water through a membrane which is permeable to both of them. In such situations, there is always the tendency of the solutes to diffuse, and the osmotic movement of water to occur, from the side of the membrane where the substance is more concentrated to the side where it is less plentiful or dilute. If this results in the salt moving outward, the water passes in the opposite direction, and vice versa. Both will always move in a direction which tends to achieve an equilibrium between the two sides of the membrane, although in biological systems the process seldom reaches equilibrium.

Diffusion (including osmosis, also a manifestation of diffusion) takes place through the atomic, ionic, molecular, or other particulate movement inherent in solutes suspended in water. It requires no energy expenditure on the part of the animal itself, and takes place with a force related to the difference between solute concentrations on the two sides of the membrane.

The problems for the fish are: (1) How to correct for the constant overloading with osmotic water coming in through the moist, soft tissues of the gills, oral cavity, etc? (If uncorrected, this would soon result in fatal "waterlogging" or overhydration and death; and (2) How to deal with the loss of salts through the same membranes in contact with environmental water. (If uncorrected, the minerals and other substances would soon be so leached out that life could no longer be sustained.) Taking in food adds some water and some salts in addition to organic materials to be processed and wastes excreted, but adds nothing major to the illustration of the osmoregulatory process presented here.

How then does the freshwater bony fish solve the problem posed?

(1) *The water problem*: The kidneys expel virtually all of the net water gained, as a copious, but very dilute urine. The water-excreting job of the kidneys would be much more demanding except for two ways in which the quantity of urine is kept within workable limits. First, the scales covering the body are impermeable to water, therefore cutting down the osmotic uptake to perhaps 1/3 of what it might be in fish without scales. Secondly, there is so much water entering the body by osmosis that it is inconceivable that these fish are ever thirsty or "drink" water, except for the small amounts they take in with their food.

(2) *The salt problem*: The fish need to conserve all the salt they can, and in addition, take in whatever more they can possibly "squeeze out" of the environmental water. The scales are as impervious to salts as they are to water. So, just as they prevent water from entering through the skin, they reduce the loss of salts from within. The kidneys not only process and expel a large volume of water, but they also cut back the loss (= wasting) of dissolved salts. The struggle to maintain water and solute content at optimum levels is aided by the gills. A large number of special chloride cells are scattered in the epithelial membranes of the gills. Those cells secrete or pump in whatever little salt is available from the environmental water into the blood, against the diffusion gradient, hence using some of the fish's own energy.

Bony fishes in salt water have internal salt concentrations that are only a little higher than the freshwater species (350 mOsm vs. 300). Whereas environmental freshwater contains near zero dissolved matter, full strength seawater contains approximately 1000 mOsm. There is neither any magical quality about seawater nor any profound physiochemical significance in the fact that seawater has an osmotic concentration of 1000 mOsm. That figure is actually the summation of the osmotic concentrations of all the components of sea water, which happens to total about 1000 in "average" full strength seawater. Furthermore, the figure varies widely in various situations, depending on many factors. For our purposes it is a convenient figure for comparing the component parts of both the surrounding water and the fish's body fluids.

Marine fishes have water and salt balance problems that are directly opposite of freshwater fishes. Sea water is a strongly dehydrating environment which threatens the resident species with being "pickled in brine." Fortunately for them, if they are in good health, they can cope very effectively. The scales covering most of the body help to keep the needed water in and the unwanted excess salt out. The kidneys produce more limited quantities of urine which is also much more concentrated with the excess salt. In order to replace the water lost by the kidneys and drawn out by osmosis, they drink seawater. The worst thing that humans adrift in a life raft can do is to drink sea water because the kidneys use more water to get rid of the salt taken in with the seawater than came in with the seawater in the first place. The bony fishes have chloride cells which "pump" the salt out across the gill linings, using some of the fish's energy just as the freshwater species do, but in the opposite direction.

Returning to the cartilaginous fishes, and more specifically the sharks, most are marine species, and the major features of their osmoregulation will be viewed first as they occur in full strength seawater with an osmotic concentration of approximately 1000 mOsm. Published figures on the body fluid composition of marine sharks vary considerably but the figures presented here are reasonably typical of reported information:

salts	575 mOsm
urea	400 mOsm
TMAO & miscellaneous	75 mOsm
Total	1050 mOsm

The salt content of shark body fluids is somewhat higher than that of the marine bony fishes (average about 575 mOsm as compared to about 350). If this were the only major constituent of the fluids, as it is for the bony fishes, the marine sharks' osmoregulatory problems would be essentially the same and they would solve their problems much as the marine bony fishes do. However, we know that elasmobranch fishes have a "urea dam" provided by special features of the gills and kidneys, and urea is retained in very high concentration. Together with TMAO and miscellaneous other substances, the total osmotic concentration of the marine shark's body fluids is slightly higher (1050 mOsm) than the 1000 mOsm of ocean water. This reverses the direction of the osmotic flow of water observed in marine bony fishes, so there is a small osmotic intake of water — just enough to provide the volume of water required for urine production. The urine is produced in relatively small quantity and although somewhat concentrated it's not as concentrated as the blood serum or seawater. Unlike bony fishes, sharks don't need to drink sea water because of this osmotic uptake of water. Nevertheless, salt taken in by diffusion through exposed surfaces and in food ingested is still too much for the kidneys alone to process. The excess salt load is discharged by two additional mechanisms, both of which were "secret weapons" until recent years.

The first, the chloride cells, were discussed in connection with the bony fishes. They and their function have been known for nearly 60 years, but whether they are also found in cartilaginous fishes has been argued since the discovery was first reported. Only within the past decade has it been demonstrated without a doubt that these cells play their expected role in removing excess salt in sharks.

The second weapon clung to its secret status considerably longer. Until 1960, the rectal gland was assigned a line or two in laboratory instruction manuals used for dogfish dissections in comparative anatomy courses. The manual I used in 1936 read, "Dorsal to the rectum is the 'rectal gland,' an elongated cylindrical structure suspended by a separate mesentery. Its function is unknown." Now we know that the gland, a supplementary salt-secreting organ, discharges virtually pure sodium chloride into the rectum, in a solution about as concentrated as in sea water. Since this discovery in 1960, there are few parts of a shark that have received more research attention than the rectal gland.

The elevated concentration of urea in elasmobranch body fluids is important to their adaptation for life in the sea. Their ability to adjust urea levels in reaction to salinity changes is the major physiological feature allowing certain species to invade brackish and even freshwater. The bull shark and the largetooth sawfish in Lake Nicaragua and its outlet, the Rio San Juan, are the most notable examples of elasmobranchs that can deal successfully with both full-strength seawater and completely freshwater, passing freely from one to the other.

When these species move more or less gradually into freshwater and stay there for a few days or more, the concentration of salts drops by about 20% and the urea by about 50%, and the internal osmotic pressure becomes about 650 mOsm, while the environmental water is near zero. This great difference between inside and outside generates a massive inward flow of water by osmosis. The flow of urine may increase as much as 20-fold, but its concentration will also be reduced by about a factor of 20, thus minimizing salt loss. Chloride cells actively pump salt into the blood from the dilute environmental water, and the rectal gland shuts down. Urea loss stops when a certain "floor" level characteristic of the species is reached. If these fish now return to the sea, the changes that occurred in freshwater will go into reverse and in a relatively short time they will return to the marine condition in all respects. On the other hand, if these fish stay in freshwater, they might well survive for a considerable time.

With few exceptions, the cartilaginous fishes (the Chondrichthyes) are the only entire class of fishes that use urea retention to regulate their water and solute balance. Only one family of stingrays, the Potamotrygonidae (the South American river rays), do not employ urea in this way. These rays live exclusively in freshwater and have lost both the urea-concentrating ability and the use of the rectal gland. Consequently they function virtually as freshwater bony fishes, and are the only elasmobranchs that live exclusively in freshwater. Their marine ancestry is evident in remnant rectal glands which are small and lack the salt-secreting function. The enzymes for urea production are present in their livers, and they actually do produce some urea. However, they have lost the "urea dam" in the gills and kidneys and are unable to build up any appreciable urea concentrations in their body fluids. They can't survive in water that is more than about 40% seawater, even when slowly acclimated to such salinity.

ADDITIONAL READING:

Baldridge, H.D., Jr. Accumulation and function of liver oil in Florida sharks. Copeia 1972 (2):306-325. (1972)

Baldridge, H.D. Sharks don't swim — they fly. Oceans 15:24-27. (1982)

Bone, Q. and B.L. Roberts. The density of elasmobranchs. Journal of the Marine Biological Association of the United Kingdom 49:913-937. (1969)

Smith, H.W. The retention and physiological role of urea in the elasmobranchii. Biological Reviews 11:49-82. (1936)

Thorson, T.B., C.M. Cowan and D.E. Watson. *Potamotrygon* spp.: elasmobranchs with low urea content. Science 158:375-377. (1967)

Thorson, T.B., C.M. Cowan and D.E. Watson. Body fluid solutes of juveniles and adults of the euryhaline bull shark *Carcharhinus leucas* from freshwater and saline environments. Physiological Zoology 46:29-42. (1973)

The Sensory World of Sharks

by ROBERT E. HUETER and PERRY W. GILBERT

They move with fluid grace through a seemingly silent world. In reality, it is a world of silence merely to the human senses. In the sensory world of sharks, the marine environment is virtually buzzing with information, transmitted over at least six different sensory channels at once. Only in recent decades have we, as alien invaders in the sea, begun to appreciate the exquisite capabilities of sharks, the sea's apex predators, to tune in to this complex sensory world.

As our own perceptions of sharks, and the lives that they lead, have changed through scientific research, so have the nicknames used to describe their remarkable sensory machinery. Once commonly called "swimming noses" — paying tribute to their highly developed sense of smell — sharks are now sometimes referred to as "swimming computers."

In reality, neither nickname is particularly accurate. "Swimming nose" sells short the other remarkable senses of sharks, perpetuating the mistaken image of primitive oafs with tiny, smell-dominated brains. And "swimming computer" overlooks what is in fact a complicated array of peripheral receptors, transforming light, sound, chemicals, and other external stimuli into internal, electrical messages — which *then* are transmitted to the integrating, analyzing "computer," the central nervous system.

Hueter is a staff scientist and manager of the Shark Biology Program at Mote Marine Laboratory where he supervises research on the anatomy, physiology, ecology, and human utilization of sharks. Gilbert was professor of neurobiology and behavior at Cornell University from 1940-1978, and executive director of Mote Marine Laboratory from 1967-1978, where he is now director emeritus. He is also a member of the Society's Advisory Council, and the author of two books and over 100 scientific papers.

This "computer" processes information from no less than six different sensory systems: hearing; olfaction (smell); vision; mechanoreception (water movement detection and touch); electroreception (sensitivity to electric fields); and taste. Depending on the strength of the stimuli, these sensory systems can detect and locate objects at varying distances, ranging from direct contact to miles away.

Sound

Sharks have no obvious external ears, and so, to the casual observer, their sense of hearing might seem rudimentary. But in fact, sharks have well-developed inner ears that respond with high sensitivity to sounds of low frequency. As in humans, the inner ear of sharks contains three semicircular canals perpendicular to one another. However, these are not the hearing organs, but rather are involved in sensing turning movements to orient the animal as it moves through the water.

The actual hearing centers lie in three chambers within the inner ear that surround organs known as maculas. These tiny organs contain specialized nerve cells, associated with small granules of calcium carbonate, that respond to sound vibrations. Two tiny pores on the top of the shark's head mark the external openings of canals which run from each inner ear to the skin surface.

The ability of sharks to hear and respond to sounds transmitted through the water has been well documented. Sharks are most responsive to, and in fact attracted by, irregularly pulsed sounds of very low frequency, particularly in the 20 to 300 Hz (cycles per second) range. This natural responsiveness tunes them in to the precise kinds of sounds made by fish that are swimming erratically, drawing their attention to more easily captured prey.

Although sharks are said to respond to sounds from distant sources, limited information is available on their natural range of hearing in the ocean. It is important to realize that such long-distance response usually requires stimuli of very high intensity at the source. Normally, such intense sounds would not be produced by typical individual prey, but may be the result of aggregate prey activities or large-scale phenomena.

Nevertheless, acoustics experts have been puzzled by sharks' remarkable abilities to home in on a distant sound source in spite of their apparent lack of the appropriate equipment. Recent studies indicate that the functioning of a fourth, "overlooked" macula in the inner ear, the macula neglecta – located beneath an opening in the skull – may be the key to providing sharks with instantaneous directional information on the source of sounds within their hearing range.

Smell

Fishermen have long known that sharks rely on a keen sense of smell to locate food. Chum, a bloody, oily blend of fish juices and parts, is commonly used to draw sharks to a bait. The chum slick provides a corridor of scent that may attract sharks from miles away, depending on sea conditions.

In the past 30 years, controlled studies at marine laboratories have established just how sensitive these animals are to certain types of chemicals in the water. Research on lemon sharks has determined that they can detect the presence of as little as 1 part of tuna extract in 25 million parts of seawater. That's equivalent to about 10 drops of extract evenly dispersed through the water in an average-sized home swimming pool. Other studies on blacktip reef and grey reef sharks have concluded that these species respond to extracts of grouper flesh in concentrations as low as 1 part per 10 billion – 1 drop in a quarter-acre lagoon 6 1/2 feet deep.

The apparatus responsible for this remarkable sensitivity lies inside the shark's nostrils, in two chambers located near the front of the snout. These nasal chambers, which are involved only in smell and not in breathing, have both incurrent and excurrent openings for more efficient flow of water through the olfactory organ. As the shark swims forward, a pressure difference is created between these openings, forcing odor-laden water to pass over the delicate sensory tissue.

Along with their hearing, sharks use this remarkable sense of smell in detecting both the presence and the location of food from a distance, as well as close up. Probably by comparing the stimulation of the two nasal chambers, as well as monitoring changes in the overall strength of a scent as they swim through the water, sharks can home in on the source of an odor with exceptional efficiency. Strong food odors can be a powerful releaser of feeding behavior in sharks, but uncontrolled "feeding frenzies" rarely occur under natural conditions.

In addition to feeding, their keen sense of smell may be involved in one other important aspect of sharks' lives — sex. There is evidence that female sharks produce sex pheromones, special chemical attractants that can stimulate male sharks to follow receptive females and engage in sexual behavior. Because it has been rare to witness the reproductive activities of sharks in captivity, this is an area of research that has just begun.

Light

The sharks' visual system faces many challenges. More than in any other sensory modality, their visual world varies in space and time, and according to their specific habitats. Some sharks live in inshore waters, others live in offshore waters, some species spend parts of their lives in both, and most operate under both daytime and nighttime conditions. So these animals must contend with broad variations in light level, visibility, color, and other optical factors.

Added to this is the fact that the visual world of many sharks is in constant motion, a result of their need to swim continuously. And for the numerous species of deep sea sharks, lack of any sort of light at all can be a real problem. Once maligned for having poor eyesight, sharks are now known to possess a well-developed visual system adapted to handle these various environmental challenges.

The shark eye is quite similar to the human eye, with a few exceptions. Like humans, but unlike most bony fishes, the shark pupil can open and close in response to varying amounts of ambient light. But since the cornea has no refractive power underwater, sharks have a thick, nearly spherical lens that provides all of the power to focus the image in the eye. In the lemon shark, for example, this lens is seven times more powerful than the human lens.

All shark retinas studied so far have both types of light-sensitive cells, the rods and cones. In general, sharks have an abundance of rods, affording them high sensitivity to light stimuli, especially under low light conditions. The chemicals that react to light in the rods are well-matched to the wavelengths of available light, even changing in some sharks as they shift habitats, so that their visual sensitivity remains topnotch. Backing up the retina is a remarkable reflective layer, the tapetum, that boosts the sensitivity of the eye even further, to where sharks may be able to detect a light dimmer than we can see.

Recent research shows that sharks also have a respectable number of cones, providing color vision capability and adequate visual acuity in their aquatic environment. In fact, some sharks, like the lemon shark, even have a specialization known as a visual streak, a higher concentration of cones and other cells in the part of the retina that scans the visual

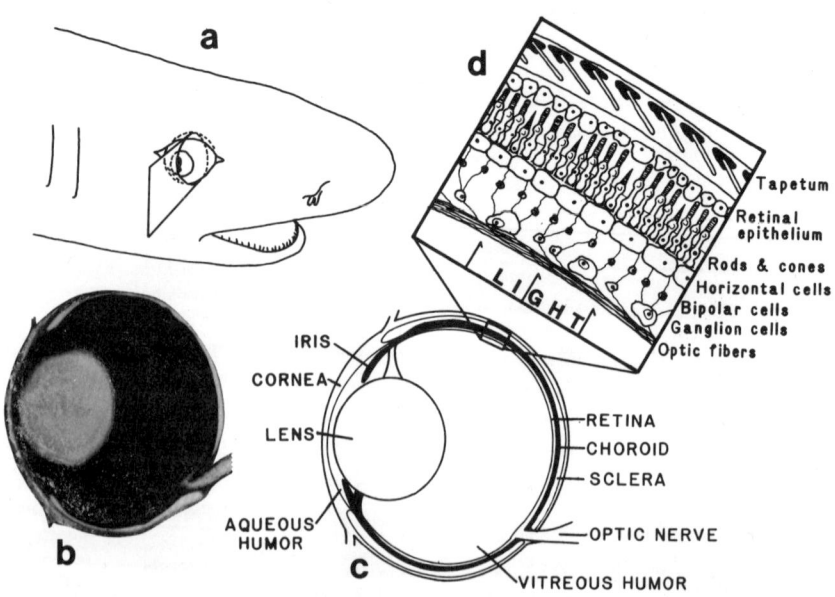

a. *Cross-section through a shark's eye.* **b.** *Frozen section of lemon shark eye (diagrammed in* **c.***)*
d. *Shark retina showing reflective tapetum in uncovered position for greater sensitivity to dim light. Rods and cones transform light into electrical signals transmitted by the ganglion cells to the brain. Drawing by R. Dixon.*

horizon. This portion of the visual field is where most of the "action" takes place for these sharks, which constantly patrol just over the sea bottom. In this way, their visual acuity is well-suited to their particular needs.

Sharks can be taught visual tasks in the laboratory, and their learning efficiency is quite good. So in their own visual world, and on their own terms, sharks can see quite well.

Water Movement and Touch

We come now to a component that is somewhat outside our own sensory experience. Although sound, smell, and light are sensations very familiar to us, the mechanical sensing of objects around us, except through direct touching, is not. As terrestrial creatures we operate in a medium of air. Rarely, though, do we sense objects in our vicinity through air movement. A passing car may send a puff of air into a pedestrian's face, providing some information on the car's proximity, speed, and direction of movement. But it is not the type of sensory information that we normally rely upon.

In the water, however, such information is commonplace. Aquatic animals are encapsulated in a dense medium capable of transmitting even the faintest movements and vibrations. This water motion, if it can be detected, represents information about the environment, and sharks do take advantage of it.

The apparatus responsible for this "distant-touch" sense is a system of mechanoreceptors distributed over the shark's body. Some of these receptors, the pit organs, are tiny, independent entities. Others are organized into a

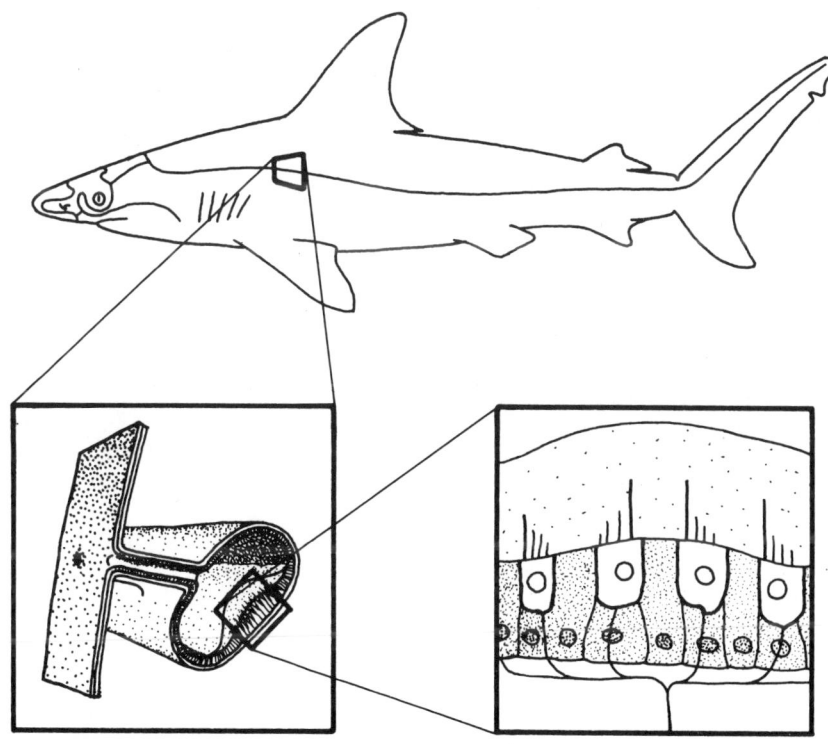

Lateral line canal (largest in a system of canals on shark's head and body, enabling it to detect objects in its vicinity) with periodic openings to the body surface. Microscopic nerve cells that detect minute vibrations, transmitting information to the brain about location of nearby objects. Drawing by R. Dixon.

branching canal system located beneath the skin of the head and body, with periodic openings to the surface. The most prominent branch of this canal system is the lateral line, which runs along each side of the body. Both pit and canal organs rely on the functioning of specialized nerve or hair cells which are sensitive to minute vibrations. Not coincidentally, hair cells are also employed in inner ear sound detection.

Understanding the anatomy and even the physiology of the mechanoreceptor system is relatively straightforward. Imagining the *sensation* it provides is not. We know that any object moving through the water creates both water displacement and compression waves; the latter relates to underwater sound and is the responsibility of the ear. The displacement of water, the actual relocation of water molecules by a moving object, is detected with extremely high sensitivity by the shark's mechanoreceptor system. This sense has a directional component that can guide the shark to the source of the disturbance.

This means that as sharks swim through the water, they somehow feel the presence and location of moving objects in their vicinity and perhaps stationary objects nearby that rebound water currents, even in the absence of all visual and auditory input. The effective range of this sense is subject to speculation, but the extreme sensitivity of the system suggests that it can operate at a fair distance from the source. How sharks separate relevant signals from the normal background disturbances is unclear, but it must be analogous to our "tuning out" background noise while trying to hear more important sounds.

In addition to this distant-touch sense, sharks also have the more human-like senses of touch, temperature detection, and possibly pain, mediated by nerve endings and corpuscles in the skin. Some of these receptors may also be involved in monitoring the shark's own body and fin movements, and specialized joint receptors provide positional information on body parts, including the jaws.

Electric Fields

Understanding the shark's mechanoreceptive sense is easy compared with grasping the nature of their "sixth sense," the ability to sense weak electric fields. Although we can build devices to detect electric fields, we do not feel the presence of weak fields around us. Sharks not only sense these fields but also rely upon them to locate prey and perhaps navigate through the ocean.

In the seawater environment, weak electric fields are generated naturally in a number of ways. Living animals produce bioelectric fields which emanate from them like an aura, or a sort of low hum — the products of muscle activity and electrochemical reactions inside the animal's body. In addition, weak electric fields are generated by movement through the earth's magnetic field, such as a shark actively swimming through the ocean, or even passively drifting in a current.

The receptors that detect these weak electric fields are concentrated in the shark's head, at the base of tiny jelly-filled canals located over the shark's snout and lower jaw, and around the eyes. Dark pores on the skin's surface mark the external openings to these sensory structures, which go by the rather lyrical name of the ampullae of Lorenzini. The ampullae contain modified nerve cells that respond to electric stimuli as faint as a few microvolts in amplitude.

Careful experimentation has demonstrated that sharks use their keen electroreceptive sense to locate prey undetectable by its other senses. For example, sharks use this sense to detect the heartbeat of a flatfish buried under the sand. Since an animal's bioelectric field drops off sharply with distance, under natural conditions, electroreception is only effective very close to the shark's head. So, sharks can invoke their sixth sense to find nearby hidden objects, to discriminate animate from inanimate objects, or to orient the head properly in executing a bite.

Hammerhead sharks have long fascinated shark biologists. A definitive exlanation of the bizarre head development has not yet been provided, but one possibility is that, driven by natural selection for more effective electroreception, the flattened head evolved to increase the electroreceptive surface. This adaptation may have resulted also in an improved directional sense of smell, due to a greater spread of the nasal chambers, as well as a hydrodynamic function. An interesting sidenote is that hammerheads appear to have a penchant for stingrays, which typically bury themselves in the sand. One can imagine them sweeping their great heads over the sea bottom, like metal detectors over sand, searching for one of their favorite foods.

Occasionally, sharks are misled by their electroreceptive sense to investigate objects that are not exactly suitable prey items like metal bars and wires that give off galvanic electric currents in seawater. Since sharks don't distinguish between natural signals and those produced by artificial man-made objects, they might appear to be "attacking" a diver's cage or boat. The shark is just doing what comes naturally.

The electroreceptive system is so sensitive that, theoretically, sharks could use it to determine their magnetic compass heading or their drift in an ocean current. Whether they actually do so has yet to be verified at sea. But if true, it would help explain how some sharks navigate during migrations over thousands of miles of ocean.

Taste

Yes, sharks do taste their food, and can discriminate between preferred and non-preferred food items. The shark's mouth and throat are lined with papillae, small mounds visible to the naked eye and containing numerous taste buds. Appeasing these taste buds is usually necessary for a final acceptance of food. Sharks will reject undesirable food items after tasting them.

Some benthic species, like the nurse

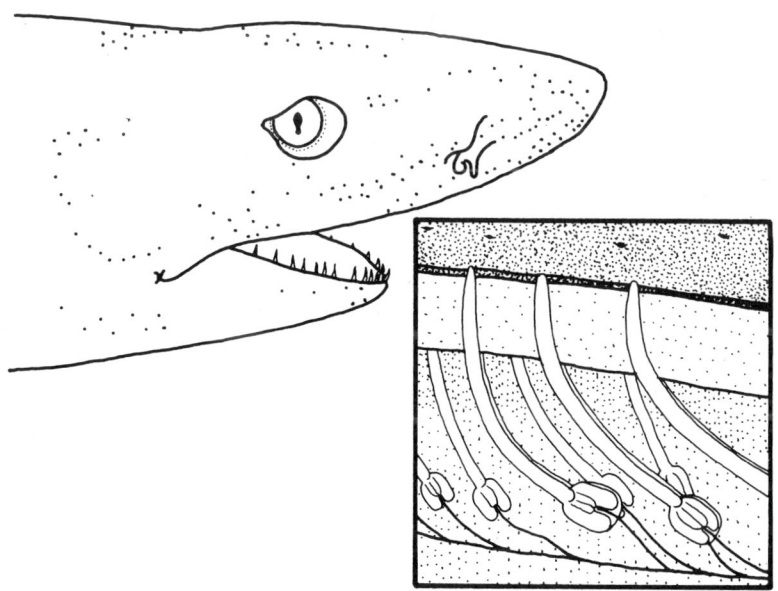

Tiny pores covering surface of shark's head leading through jelly-filled canals to electrosensitive ampullae of Lorenzini. Drawing by R. Dixon.

shark, are equipped with mouth barbels. These presumably have a taste function and may come into play as the sharks root around the bottom and in holes, searching for bottom-dwelling invertebrates and fishes.

Since nearly all sharks are restricted to seawater, they must somehow be sensitive to a drop in salinity if they enter estuarine or fresh water. It is unknown whether they have a sensory system that monitors salinity, or they simply react to a salinity decrease through their gills or other tissues, but certainly the sense of taste could be involved.

Inside the Shark Brain

Comprehending what is perceived inside an animal's head is one of the great challenges of comparative neuroscience and psychology. It is difficult enough to imagine the sensory perceptions of the family dog, much less a shark. All we can really hope to do is study the anatomy, physiology, and behavior of an animal, draw comparisons with other species including ourselves, and make predictions about how the animal will respond to certain sensory stimuli.

Sharks have been stereotyped as unpredictable. As the results of scientific research have accumulated over the past 40 years, it is evident that sharks respond to sensory stimuli and behave as they do for very good reasons — primarily to fulfill their role as apex predators in the sea.

Sensory information about the environment is brought into the shark's brain, analyzed, integrated, and acted upon. Their brains are large, comparable in relative size to those of birds and mammals. The primary targets for sensory information are in the shark's forebrain for smell, the midbrain for vision, and the hindbrain for hearing, mechanoreception, electroreception, and taste.

But it isn't quite that simple. Auxiliary pathways and centers of sensory integration exist in shark brains, as in the human brain, where information from several sensory channels can be compared. For example, the shark's large forebrain, which was once thought to be devoted entirely to smell, is now known to receive visual information through pathways from the midbrain. And the shark's midbrain structure known as the optic tectum (optic for its visual role, and the Latin word tectum meaning "roof" for its rooflike shape) actually receives overlapping input from both the visual world and the electric world. Perhaps such sensory overlaps allow sharks to make even finer discriminations about the nature and location of objects in their environment.

Some experiments indicate that a kind of sensory hierarchy exists in the shark brain, allowing certain types of sensory information to receive greater attention than others. A shark will veer away from an odoriferous piece of food to bite at a pair of electrodes, or even a metal bar, which is simulating a natural bioelectric

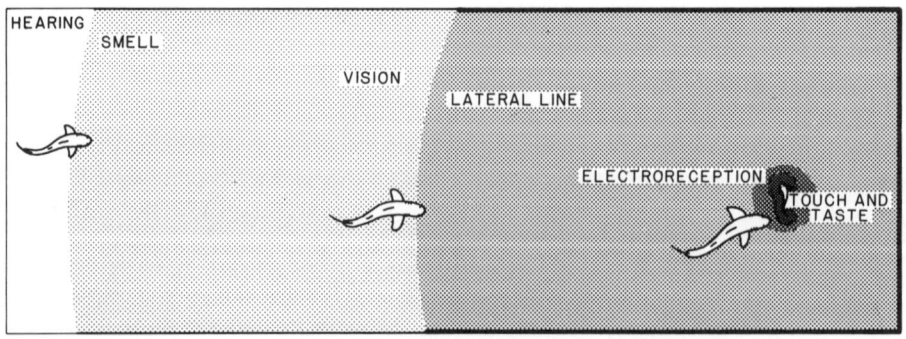

Various senses are stimulated at different distances as shark approaches, or is approached by, an object.

field, as if the electric signal overrides the olfactory one. In this way, the shark typically responds with time-tested efficiency to the most relevant stimuli in its environment. Only under usually man-made, artificial conditions do things go awry.

The distances away from a shark at which these various senses operate have been vigorously debated. Quite often the physical limitations of the aquatic realm set the limits of operation, rather than the physiological or behavioral limitations of the shark. For example, there is no reason to believe that sharks cannot see to the edge of underwater visibility, which may range from one to 100 feet depending upon their particular habitat. Theoretically, sounds and odors can be detected by sharks miles away from the source, but the strength of the stimulus at the source must be intense to do so. The only senses with fixed ranges are taste and touch, which operate strictly on direct contact.

Nevertheless, in the everyday sensory world of sharks, each of the six senses is brought into play at varying distances from normal sources of stimuli. Hearing and smell can alert a shark to an item out of visual range, and help guide the shark toward it. Lateral line and vision may come into play next, providing more precise information on the spatial location of the item. Electroreception and taste join the other four senses at the end of the approach, helping to resolve the item's position and identity.

Although we can never truly know what goes on inside a shark's head, we can make the effort to view its world through the shark's own eyes, ears, and other senses. Only then will we begin to appreciate just how remarkable these creatures truly are.

ADDITIONAL READING:

Cohen, J.L. 1981. Vision in sharks. Oceanus 24:17-22.

Gilbert, P.W. 1984. Biology and behavior of sharks. Endeavour, New Series 8:179-187.

Gruber, S.H. 1977. The visual systems of sharks: adaptations and capability. American Zoologist 17:453-469.

Hodgson, E.S. and R.F. Mathewson (eds.). 1978. Sensory Biology of Sharks, Skates, and Rays. U.S. Govt. Printing Office, Washington, DC.

Kalmijn, A.J. and K.J. Rose. 1978. The shark's sixth sense. Natural History 87:76-81.

Montgomery, J.C. 1988. Sensory physiology. In Physiology of Elasmobranch Fishes, ed. by T.J. Shuttleworth, pp. 79-98. Springer-Verlag, Berlin.

Whitetip reef shark. Photo by J. Stafford-Deitsch.

SHARK REPRODUCTION:
Parental Investment and Limited Fisheries, An Overview

by HAROLD L. PRATT, JR. and JOSÉ I. CASTRO

The responses of living organisms to the problems of survival have produced a myriad of fascinating solutions.

Sharks and their relatives, the skates and rays, are successful as a group because of many factors. Probably the most important, is the development of remarkably efficient reproductive strategies including internal fertilization, maternal nourishment of embryos, and the birth of large young that are well-developed miniatures of the adults, often up to three feet long and weighing 30 to 40 pounds.

Unlike most other fishes, sharks as a group employ internal fertilization through copulation and produce small quantities of large young. Internal fertilization permits the development of several interesting and diverse modes of reproduction.

Primitive sharks usually lay eggs (OVIPARITY). Developing embryos are dependent solely on the yolk reserves within their eggs. This type of oviparity is different from that of bony fishes. The eggs are large for fish eggs (1 to 2 inches), well supplied with yolk, and protected by

Oviparous embryo of chain dogfish removed from the egg case. Photo by J.I. Castro

Pratt has worked on shark life history for over 20 years with the Apex Predators Investigation at the National Marine Fisheries Service Laboratory, Narragansett, RI. Castro is a shark biologist with the NMFS Laboratory, Miami, FL, and wrote THE SHARKS OF NORTH AMERICAN WATERS.

a tough shell. The shell also permits attachment to the substrate and embryonic respiration. The eggs must survive unguarded for weeks or months until they hatch. Parental care is unknown in elasmobranchs. The hatchlings are small compared to the non-ovoviviparous sharks since they are limited by the amount of yolk reserves in the egg. For instance a newborn whale shark may emerge from the egg at 14 inches. The adult is the largest fish in the ocean, reaching at least 40 feet.

A more advanced reproductive strategy is the maintenance of relatively large embryos in the uterus until development is complete. When the embryos do not form a placenta, the developmental process is called OVOVIVIPARITY, or APLACENTAL VIVIPARITY by modern authors. This is the most common reproductive strategy in sharks, affording shelter from predation and environmental hazards, and producing large embryos. It reduces numbers of young in favor of larger newborn with a greater chance of survival. The embryos are nourished by yolk stored in a yolk sac attached directly to their digestive system. The dogfish sharks, cow sharks, frill sharks, angel sharks, tiger sharks, and some nurse sharks are a few of the many ovoviviparous species.

Maternal reproductive investment per embryo in ovoviviparous sharks is greatest in species that have developed OOPHAGY. In this mode, the young hatch within the uterus in the first three months of gestation and consume eggs which the female continues to ovulate throughout gestation. The lamnoid sharks, makos, white sharks, threshers, crocodile sharks, sand tigers, and false catsharks, are known to be oophagous. The sand tiger shark is in fact EMBRYOPHAGOUS in that the first embryo to hatch within the uterus attacks and consumes its siblings before settling down to a diet of maternal eggs (see Gilmore, this issue).

The most complex form of shark reproduction, PLACENTAL VIVIPARITY (see Hamlett this issue), is employed by the requiem and hammerhead sharks. These advanced families have developed a maternal nutrient system very similar to the one found in mammals. After a short period of embryonic dependence on the yolk sac, the empty, flaccid yolk sac interdigitates with the maternal uterine wall to form a yolk sac placenta. The embryo is supported at the end of an umbilical cord which enters its body between the pectoral fins. The placenta transports resources from the mother's bloodstream, including nutrients and oxygen supply, and provides elimination of waste products.

In some viviparous sharks, such as the sharpnose and some of the hammerheads, additional structures are present. The umbilical cord becomes festooned with "appendicula," leaf-like structures that increase the umbilical cord's surface area for exchange of nutrients, gases, and waste products with the uterine fluid. "Uterine milk," secreted by special cells in the walls of the uterus of these sharks, may be absorbed through the extended gill filaments of many species of elasmobranchs, as well as the appendicula, and the skin and mouths of the embryos.

Along with these varied reproductive strategies, sharks have developed some unique organs and anatomical features.

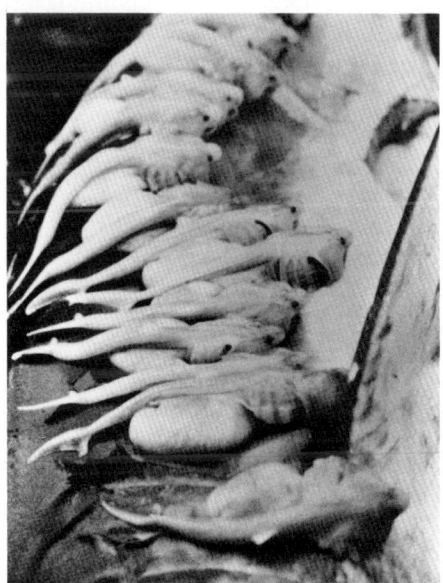

Viviparous, oophagous, embryos (about 16 inches long) taken from a 735 lb. shortfin mako caught off Alabama in 1978.

A single ovary, usually the right, is large and invested with dozens to sometimes thousands of large, yolky eggs. Ovaries can be of two forms, with eggs developed and dispatched from the surface of the gland, or as a tissue mass with a central cavity from which eggs escape through pores. Eggs enter the oviduct through a funnel-shaped ostium and pass down into the paired oviducts through the shell gland where sperm is stored in some species and fertilization sometimes occurs. The shell gland also secretes a protective covering, either tough, flexible, and thick as in the whale shark, or thin and transparent as in the blue shark. The oviducts end in paired uteri where the embryos develop in viviparous species.

The number of embryos born to a single mother varies from two (bigeye thresher, sand tiger) to 135 (blue shark). Gestation lasts from three or four months in small sharks to two years in the spiny dogfish and perhaps longer for the frilled shark. A period of nine to 12 months is typical of most large sharks. The young usually emerge tail first; although some species, like the sand tiger, are born head first. "Tee-shaped" heads of young hammerheads are soft and pliable at birth to permit easy passage through the birth canal. Sharks give birth in a variety of habitats from the deep ocean floor to coral reef environments, but many seek out shallow, near-shore waters, or estuaries, because of the abundant food supply and absence of most large predators. Any environmental degradation of coastal areas, however, threatens the nursery area of even these nomadic ocean dwellers.

The age of sexual maturity for sharks is difficult to determine, and consequently not well known. Unlike the bony fishes that often grow quite rapidly and mature in just a few years, most species of sharks grow slowly and take many years to reach maturity. The larger requiem sharks usually mature in six to 18 years, or longer, depending on the species. The maximum ages and years of reproductive life for these sharks can only be guessed. Current age research indicates that the largest individuals landed are 30 to 40 years old. Evidence suggests that certain dogfish species can live 70 years.

Many of the large shark species reproduce every other year. A female sandbar shark giving birth this spring will not mate again until the following spring; then it will gestate for about a year and give birth the next spring. Many females are thin and emaciated when they reach full term. Alternate year pupping may be required for the female to store sufficient nutrients to pass to the offspring. Some species such as the blue, hammerhead,

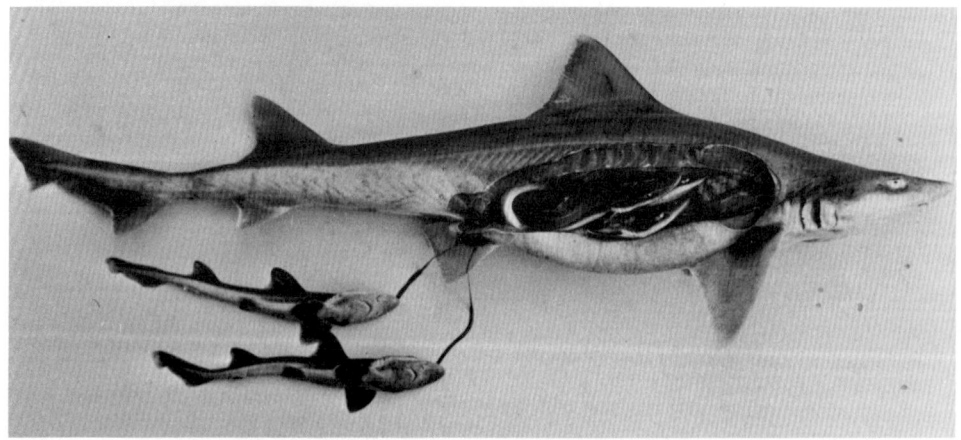

Placentally viviparous smalleye smoothhound. Photo by J.I. Castro.

Umbilical cord and placenta of the smooth dogfish. Photo by J.I. Castro.

sand tiger, and sharpnose sharks reproduce every year, as do most of the egg-laying species.

Male sharks are as reproductively complex as the females. Internal fertilization is accomplished using one or both claspers, which are rod-like appendages of the male's pelvic fins. Claspers are rotated and inserted into the female's vagina after a sometimes elaborate but poorly known courtship process in which the male bites the female's fins and flanks until she is receptive. The maneuvering to permit copulation must be complex, especially with females weighing thousands of pounds. The clasper is anchored in the female by terminal spurs or sharpened expandable ridges and spermatozoa are transferred in a stream of water driven by paired siphon sacs. These sacs are a muscle-driven hydraulic system in the abdominal wall of the males. All of this rough interplay with teeth and spurs has been softened over the eons by the development of thicker skin in female sharks. The skin of the adult female blue shark, for example, is three times thicker than the male's – thicker than the length of his teeth.

Sperm is produced in small, round sacs or ampullae in two large testes located far forward, deep in the male body cavity. It is stored as thousands of sperm packets, dense pellets of aligned spermatozoa, formed and held in large vesicles at the very end of the reproductive tract. Thus, male sharks are prepared to deliver large quantities of sperm to the female when chances of reproductive success are highest. In some sharks, the females can store sperm for years, another tactic for ensuring fertilization in the uncertain life of a migratory animal.

The interplay of all of these factors enhances the success of fertilization and survival of the young. However, these strategies work against sharks when they are harvested by man. The high maternal investment in each embryo means a very low rate of reproduction. Sharks

Appendicula of the bonnethead shark. Photo by J.I. Castro.

propagate by two's and four's, dozens at most. These small numbers are enough to keep up with natural mortality, but not large enough to keep pace with human predation. Little is known about the resilience of sharks under these circumstances. In some animal populations, fecundity of individuals increases when the populations size decreases. The evidence of collapsed fisheries for threshers, porbeagles, school sharks, dogfish, and other species indicates that sharks lack the resilience to adapt to intensive harvesting. Because of these reproductive strategies and the limitations and unknowns surrounding them, we must be conservative in harvesting these fragile shark populations.

ADDITIONAL READING:

Castro, J.I. THE SHARKS OF NORTH AMERICAN WATERS. Texas A & M. 1983.

Hoar, W.S., D.J. Randall, and E.M. Donaldson. FISH PHYSIOLOGY, Vol. IX. Reproduction. Parts A & B, Academic Press. 1983.

Springer, Victor G. and Joy P. Gold. SHARKS IN QUESTION. Smithsonian Institution Press. 1989.

Wourms, John P. Reproduction and development in chondrichthyan fishes. American Zoologist, Vol. 17, No. 2 p. 379-410.

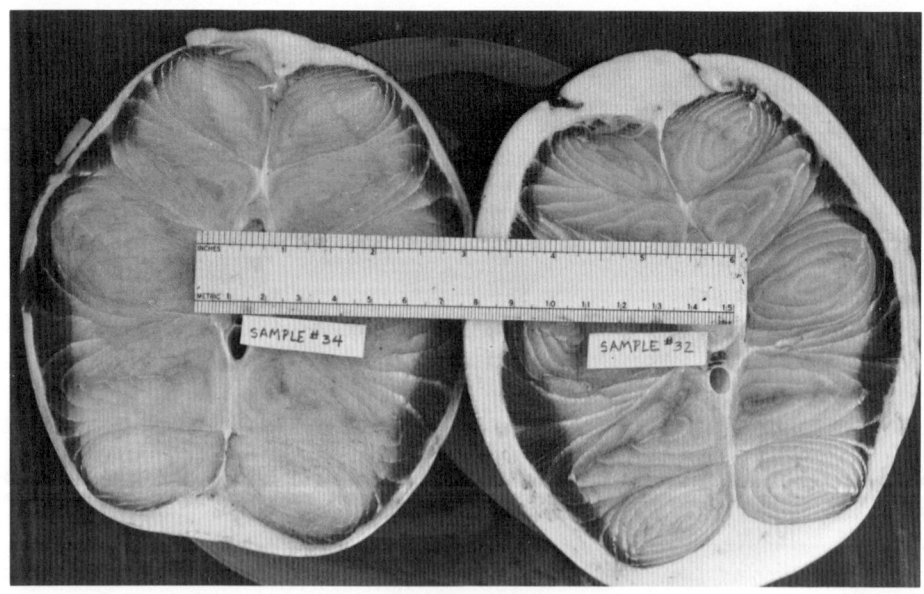

Cross sections of two blue sharks (female, right; male, left) showing sexually dimorphic skin thickness. Photo H. W. Pratt.

From Egg to Placenta: Placental Reproduction in Sharks

by WILLIAM C. HAMLETT

There are three major methods used by vertebrates to nourish their developing offspring. The first is yolk reserves, the most familiar example being the chicken egg. The embryo relies entirely on the yolk supply for the nutrients it needs during development. The second method involves uterine secretion of nutrient substances called histotroph or "uterine milk," a kind of maternal milk shake. The embryo ingests or absorbs this material for its nutrient demands. This method of nutrient delivery is best developed in the stingrays. The final method is through the placenta. Fetal membranes form a connection with maternal tissues producing a uteroplacental complex that supplies the embryo with nutrients and oxygen and removes wastes. Generally, a single species utilizes one or two of these methods; however, placental sharks utilize all three, progressing from reliance on yolk, to dependence on histotroph, to a placenta during their gestation periods. Sharks are ancient animals, evolving some 350 million years ago, yet, they display a fantastic array of very successful "modern" reproductive methods to insure the birth of viable young.

Approximately 70% of all sharks give birth to live young. Of these approximately 30% are placental and develop a placenta analogous to that of mammals. Although the embryonic origin and the fetal membranes involved are different than in mammals, the same basic functions of uterine incubation and maintenance of physiological equilibrium are served.

As noted, there are many similarities in the basic reproductive mechanisms of sharks and higher vertebrates. All male sharks fertilize the females internally by means of modified pelvic fins called claspers. The same reproductive hormones active in man are also present in sharks. Embryos of placental sharks develop in the uterus of the mother and receive nourishment during a prolonged pregnancy, generally 8-12 months. The babies are born alive and are capable of swimming and hunting independently at birth in an often hostile marine environment.

Aristotle made the first observations on shark reproduction and was aware that some were placental while others were egg layers. He also knew that the sharks practiced internal fertilization but incorrectly called the sexual apparatus of males "claspers" because he thought the male held the female with these fin elements.

Characteristics of placental sharks include: 1) a lengthy gestation period, 2) a reduced number of offspring when compared to bony fishes, 3) an increased degree of maternal protection during the development of the embryos, and 4) increased chance of survival of the offspring due to their large size at birth.

In humans multiple births are considered unusual; in sharks it is the rule. Placental sharks bear from four to over 100 offspring depending on the species. While these numbers seem impressive by human standards, they are modest compared to the thousands of eggs a trout may lay at one time — relatively few of which will successfully survive. Since the shark embryos are safely incubated in the

On the faculty of the Medical College of Ohio in Toledo, Hamlett has organized special international symposia on elasmobranchs. His research specialization involves the evolution of viviparity and reproductive biology of elasmobranchs.

mother's uterus, virtually all survive to birth. Sharks have few natural enemies, and the mother's ability to carry her offspring protects them from predation.

Initially the embryo is attached by a yolk stalk to the egg mass enclosed in the yolk sac. Yolk is transported up the yolk stalk to supply the embryo with nutrients.

placenta pushes against the wall of the uterus to establish a placental connection with the mother. Both the fetal and maternal portions of the placental complex are richly supplied with a profusion of blood vessels. The shark fetuses are nourished by the food in the mother's blood in a manner similar to but not

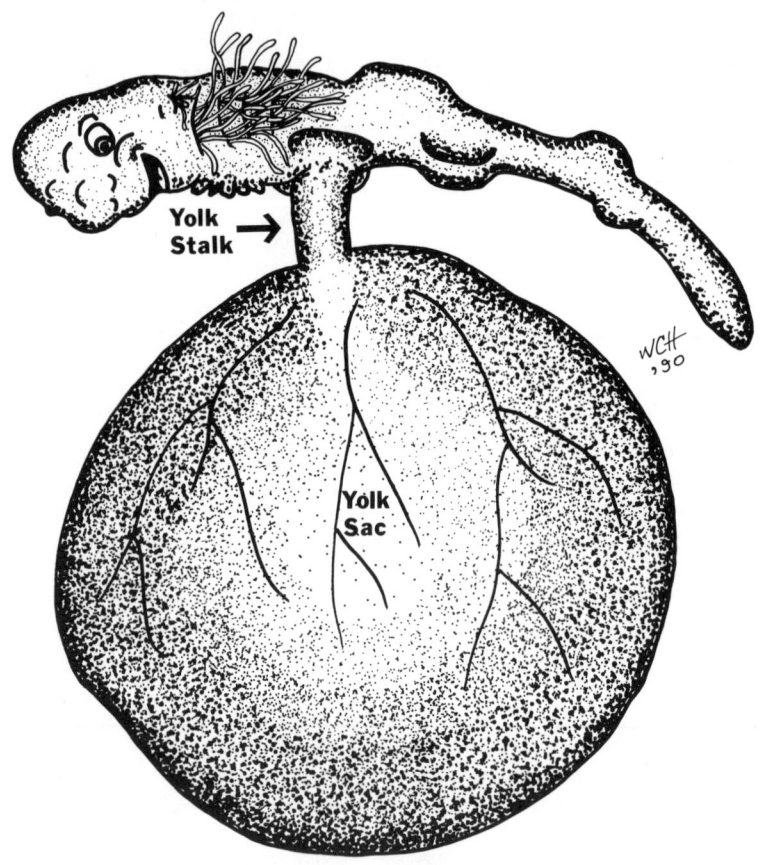

Yolk-reliant embryo. Drawing by W. Hamlett.

Near mid-pregnancy, as the yolk supplies are depleted, the maternal uterus elaborates a protein rich uterine milk to supplement the yolk supplies. The embryos ingest the uterine milk and may also absorb it. Next the yolk sac undergoes complex structural and functional conversion into a placenta. The old yolk stalk is now called an umbilical cord, for it connects the baby to the mother. The

exactly the same as that of humans. At parturition, or birth, the pups are delivered one at a time. The umbilical cord breaks and leaves a small scar, the equivalent of a belly button, between the pectoral fins.

Current and future studies of placental sharks and the basic mechanisms of nutrient transfer will shed light on these process in vertebrates in general.

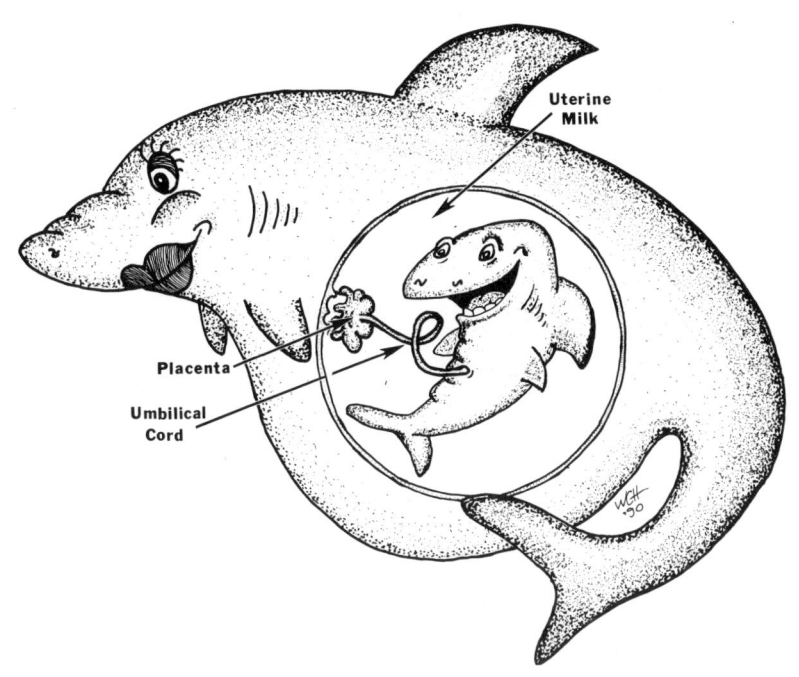

Mother shark and fetus. Drawing by W. Hamlett.

ADDITIONAL READING:

Budker, P. 1971. THE LIFE OF SHARKS, Columbia University Press, New York.

Hamlett, W.C. and B. Tota (eds.). 1989. Evolutionary and Contemporary Biology of Elasmobranchs, J. Exper. Zool., Suppl. 2, 200 pp., Alan R. Liss, Inc., New York.

Lineweaver, T.H. and R.H. Backus. 1970. THE NATURAL HISTORY OF SHARKS, Andre Deutsch Limited, London.

A term Atlantic sharpnose shark fetus with umbilical cord connecting placenta. Photo by W. Hamlett.

The Reproductive Biology of Lamnoid Sharks

by R. GRANT GILMORE

Lamnoid or mackerel sharks belong to the order Lamniformes consisting of 16 species in seven families. The sand tiger sharks (4 species), goblin sharks (1 species), crocodile sharks (1 species), megamouth sharks (1 species), thresher sharks (3 species), basking sharks (1 species), and mackerel sharks (5 species) form a group of basically pelagic species whose life history and reproductive biology have been extremely difficult to study.

Just nine species in four families have been captured during pregnancy, and little detailed reproductive information has been derived from seven of these species. Only the sand tiger shark (*Odontaspis taurus*, also known as the ragged tooth in South Africa or grey nurse in Australia), has been studied in detail from the moment of ovum fertilization to birth. All species within the order captured during pregnancy were found to have egg-eating embryos. All of these species except the thresher sharks, *Alopias* spp., and the sand tiger, have multiple embryos of nearly identical size within a single uterus. The shortfin mako, *Isurus oxyrinchus*, may have up to nine embryos in a single uterus. Although egg-eating or oophagy has been well documented, there is no evidence for embryonic cannibalism in these species. Only the sand tiger shark is a documented intrauterine cannibal.

Embryonic oophagy in lamnoid sharks is an efficient means of increasing growth, and producing a relatively large

Gilmore has conducted research in ichthyology and fish ecology with the Harbor Branch Oceanographic Institution, Ft. Pearce, FL, since 1971. Shark study began there in 1975 with an inshore population survey off Melbourne, FL. The embryology of all lamnoid sharks has been under study since 1976.

embryo at birth (parturition). These large young have a size advantage allowing for predation on other fishes and for escape from the mostly smaller predaceous fishes. Embryos of porbeagles, makos, threshers, and sand tigers range from 67 to 110 cm (26 to 43 inches) at birth, while unverified records of 170 cm (67 inches) basking shark embryos are in the literature. However, the functional significance of sand tiger shark embryos hunting and consuming other embryos within the uterus leaving only one per uterus to survive remains an enigma.

The detailed study of reproduction in the sand tiger shark has provided considerable information and reveals a developmental pattern unique among elasmobranchs. Sand tiger populations studied in the most detail are those occurring along the coast of North America from Cape Hatteras to Florida. I have studied the reproductive biology of east Florida populations for 15 years, and the following analyses are derived from these studies, much of which has been published.

Female and male sand tigers rendezvous at specific mating sites in relatively shallow water (30 to 60 m or 98 to 197 foot depths) each spring from March to May, from Florida to North Carolina. The time varies depending on latitude, occurring earlier in Florida waters. Females give birth during the winter, one to two months prior to this rendezvous. All mature females examined to date from the Florida populations were impregnated at approximately the same time. The mating activity is so predictable that embryonic development is also predictable and females captured throughout the year contain embryos in the same stage of development. For example up to nine females captured on the same set line contained 18 embryos measuring nearly the same length indicating synchronous development. No mature, unimpregnated females have been collected between the months of March and January, indicating that sand tiger sharks are impregnated every year and spend the majority of their adult lives carrying ravenous developing embryos in two uteri. After mating, males leave for an unknown location, most likely deeper waters offshore.

Encapsulated ova consistently occur in the oviducal gland around sunrise, indicating that ovulation occurs every 24 hours. Fertilization apparently takes place when ova enter the ostium since in recently mated female sand tigers live sperm have been isolated from the ostium and entire oviduct. Initial ovulations release two ova, a single ovum per oviduct. Successive ovulations release two, three, then multiple ova per oviduct simultaneously. The position and number of the ova and egg capsules is often the same in either oviduct, indicating that the ova enter the oviducts alternately but nearly simultaneously. After encapsulation in the oviducal gland, the developing embryos move down the oviduct, through the isthmus, and into the uterus. The initial embryo to develop is alone in its capsule. Subsequent embryos may have from one to 15 companions since fertilization of multiple ovulations appears to take place over one to two weeks. After this period multiple ovulations may fill the egg capsules with up to 18 ova, but they are no longer fertilized.

The early development of sand tiger embryos more closely resembles the development of amphibians, frogs, newts, and salamanders than the development of other sharks. Yolk fills the heart and coelomic cavities and distends the abdominal cavity of the 13 mm (.5 inch) total length (TL) embryo. A yolk sac is attached to the abdomen by a yolk stalk. The developing embryo uses yolk from both sources. At 50 to 60 mm (2-2.5 inches TL) the embryo develops large teeth and has an optic filament attached to the orbit along with well developed filaments exiting the spiracle and gill slits. These filaments undoubtedly increase oxygen transport to the rapidly growing embryonic tissues.

At 60 mm (2.5 inches TL) the first embryo to develop tears through the elastic collagen membrane of its egg capsule and enters the uterus. It then consumes the remaining yolk from its yolk sac and may derive some nutrition from the uterine fluid bathing the intrauterine space. At 100 mm (4 inches) the embryo begins to hunt for egg capsules containing other embryos. Even though many capsules may be present in the uterus, only those containing embryos are damaged by the first embryo in this phase. In Florida sand tiger populations embryonic cannibalism begins in July. The first embryo rips the egg capsule membrane or punctures it with its teeth, often killing the embryo inside well before the capsule is opened. After the other siblings are removed from their respective capsules they are consumed. Four embryos 9 to 36 mm (.3-1.5 inches TL) were found in the pharynx of a single 334 mm (13 inch) embryo. None of these were digested, indicating recent consumption.

By the time it reaches 350 mm (14 inches TL), all the other embryos have been consumed, and this remaining embryo gorges on egg capsules containing unfertilized ova. By October, the embryo's stomach and abdominal wall are distended grotesquely beyond normal body proportions, giving the impression that the embryo has consumed a soccer ball. However, a month before parturition the mother's ovary has declined considerably in size, ovulation ceases, and the embryo's abdominal contour returns to normal in spite of an enlarged liver. At birth the 100 cm (40 inch) embryo resembles a miniature adult, though not as robust. Thus only two embryos are produced, one from each uterus. Birth has taken place in captivity

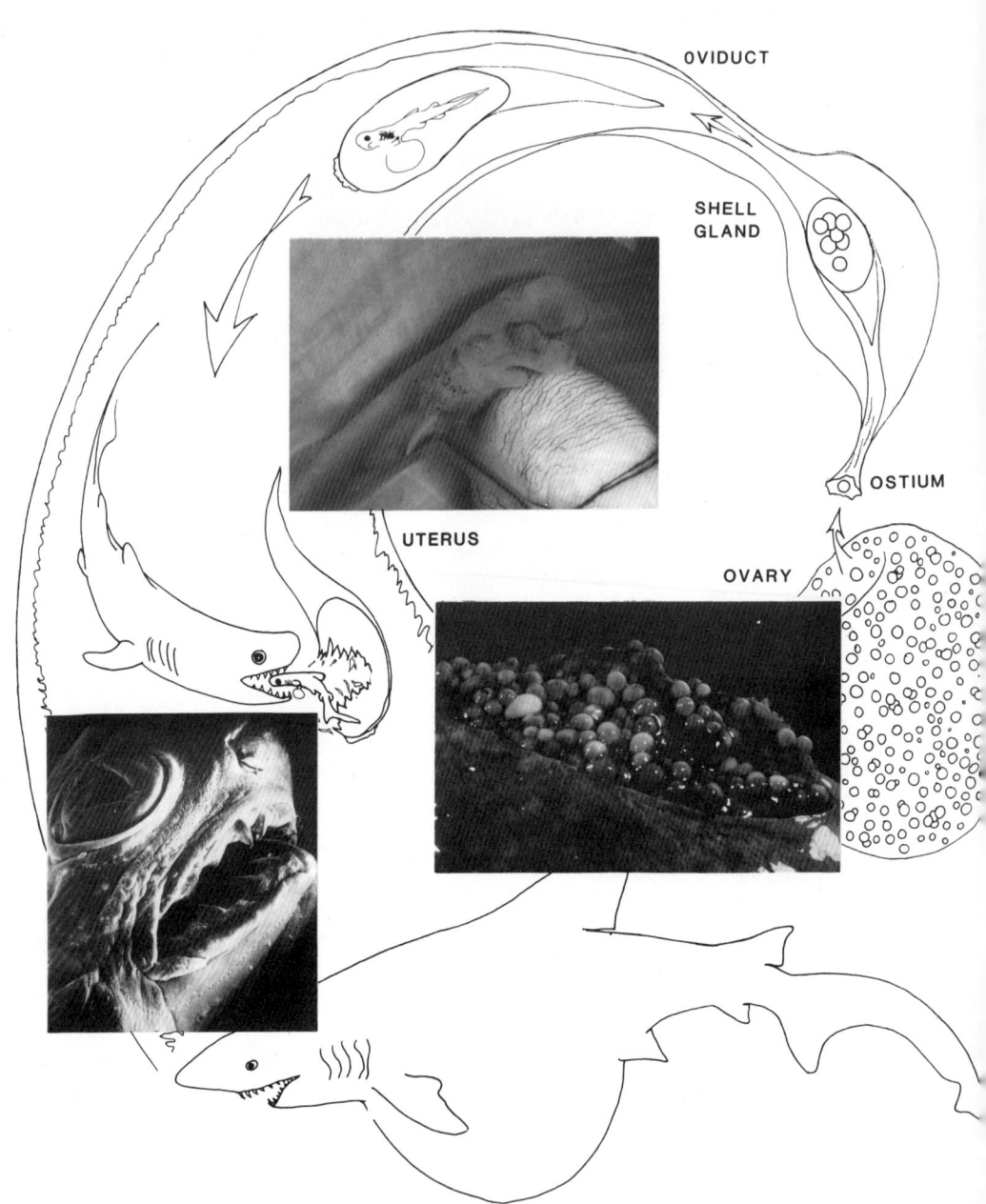

*Nine months of embryonic development in the sand tiger shark.
Ovulation and fertilization of a 10 mm (0.4 inches) egg in anterior oviduct near the ostium; egg encapsulation in the shell gland; embryonic cannibalism; and completion of egg eating (oophagous) stage showing embryo with distended stomach. A month or two after last egg capsule is eaten, embryo reaches 40 inches in length and is born. Drawing by R.G.Gilmore.*

on several occasions and in February 1959 was documented on film at Marineland, Florida. During parturition the young sand tigers emerged snout first, upside down and swam to the water's surface to take a bubble of air into the stomach cavity. (Surface air gulping is also a common behavior in adult sand tigers but its function is unknown.)

The functional significance of intrauterine cannibalism in the sand tiger shark has not been determined. Other lamnoid sharks give birth to up to 18 embryos which provides them a distinct numerical advantage over the sand tiger shark even though both have experienced rapid growth rates through oophagy. A sand tiger pup born in captivity killed a leopard shark,*Triakis semifasciata,* in the same aquarium only 24 days after birth. This indicates that post parturition sand tigers are aggressive but does not reveal how aggressive compared to other lamnoid or carcharhinid sharks of similar size at birth. Until comparative behavioral experiments are conducted with captive newborn sand tigers and carcharhinid sharks, the adaptive significance of in-utero sibling rivalry will remain a mystery.

ADDITIONAL READING:

Gilmore, R.G. 1983. Observations on the embryos of the longfin mako, *Isurus paucus*, and the bigeye thresher, *Alopias superciliosus*. Copeia 1983:375-382.

Gilmore, R.G., J.W. Dodrill and P.A. Linley, 1983. Embryonic development of the sand tiger shark, *Odontaspis taurus* Rafinesque. Fish. Bull., 81:201-225.

Gruber, S.H., and L.J.V. Compagno. 1982. Taxonomic status and biology of the bigeye thresher, *Alopias superciliosus*. Fish. Bull., 79:617-640

Ellis, R. 1976.. THE BOOK OF SHARKS. Grosset and Dunlop, NY.

Stevens, J.D. 1983. Observations on reproduction in the shortfin mako *Isurus oxyrinchus*. Copeia 1983:126-130.

NEED MORE INFORMATION ABOUT DISCOVERING SHARKS?

The following organizations work on shark research and conservation:

Jeffrey C. Carrier, Sec./Editor
American Elasmobranch Society
Department of Biology
Albion College
Albion, MI 49224

Harold Upton
Fisheries Program Director
Center for Marine Conservation
1725 DeSales Street, NW
Washington, DC 20036

Jack Casey
Apex Predator Investigation
National Marine Fisheries Service
28 Tarzwell Drive
Narragansett, RI 02882-1199

John West
Conservation Center
The Taronga Zoo
Mosman, Sydney
New South Wales, Australia

Australian Conservation Foundation
18 Argyle Place
The Rocks 2000
New South Wales, Australia

International Shark Attack File
Florida Museum of Natural History
University of Florida
Gainesville, FL 32611

Samuel H. Gruber, Chairman, Shark Specialist Committee
Species Survival Commission of IUCN / The World Conservation Union
Bimini Biological Station / UM
4600 Rickenbacker Causeway
Miami, FL 33149-1098

GROWTH AND AGING:
Life History Studies of the Nurse Shark

by JEFFREY C. CARRIER

Commonly encountered in the shallow, nearshore waters of the southern United States and the tropical regions of the Caribbean Sea and southwestern Atlantic Ocean, nurse sharks, *Ginglymostoma cirratum*, are frequently the first

Because of their docile nature and ability to thrive in captivity, nurse sharks appear in many marine exhibits. Unlike many shark species which must swim to breathe, nurse sharks can rest on the bottom which makes them particularly

Nurse shark tagging in the Florida Keys provides important clues about growth and aging in this common, shallow-water shark. Photo by R. Beech.

and perhaps the only sharks encountered by visitors to the coast. Rarely considered dangerous, these animals are common sights for divers and fishermen alike. They are slow moving, and their dark color makes them easy to spot in shallow water.

Associate professor and chairman of the Department of Biology, Albion College, Albion, MI, Carrier has studied salt and water balance in nurse sharks and freshwater stingrays. His recent work involves nurse shark aging, growth, and movements in the Florida Keys.

suitable for laboratory research. Literally hundreds of papers have been published covering virtually all aspects of their biology, their ability to learn and remember, their physiological adaptations for limited survival in freshwater, and their resistance to certain types of cancer.

The very characteristics which make nurse sharks so useful may ultimately threaten their existence. Though of little commercial value as a food source, they are commonly sought for crab trap bait or simply for the "sport" of killing sharks.

Slow moving and relatively easy to capture, they are not well endowed with large, cutting teeth, and seem to have few defense mechanisms.

In recent years, we have begun to examine the life history of this species in more detail. We learned that their growth rate is, like many shark species, very slow. They may grow only 13 centimeters (5 inches) per year and gain a mere 2-3 kilograms (4-7 pounds). Larger nurse shark specimens have measured 400 centimeters (13 feet), suggesting quite a long life span. These growth rates vary, as 13 centimeters per year represents an average, but we know that juveniles grow at somewhat faster rates than adults.

Young nurse sharks apparently range very little. In our tagging study conducted around Big Pine Key in the Florida Keys, we have recaptured nearly 30% of the tagged animals. Many were recaptured several times, some within days and some as long as three years after the initial tagging. Most of these are recaptured from the same restricted area. This suggests that nurse sharks range very little or that they return faithfully to the same area. Our work with ultrasonic tracking tags shows that daily movements are also minimal. One animal we tracked for 96 consecutive hours moved less than one mile. As they grow larger, however, nurse sharks seem to move greater distances, a characteristic common to other species in these areas including lemon sharks, *Negaprion brevirostris*.

We believe that this increased range in larger nurse sharks may coincide with the onset of sexual maturity. Males are sexually mature when they reach around 210 centimeters in total length (82 inches). Females mature sexually at lengths around 240 centimeters (94 inches). When these figures are examined with respect to growth rates, the data suggest that males may be 10 to 15 years old before they can reproduce and females may be 15 to 20 years old.

Slow growing animals like nurse sharks require many years to reach reproductive age, reproduce infrequently, and do not produce hundreds of offspring, so they are generally at some risk from environmental pressures. As commercial pressures increase or sport fishing demands continue, nurse sharks, as well as many other shark species, may be at an even greater risk unless management initiatives are considered and implemented to maintain viable shark populations.

ADDITIONAL READING:

Carrier, J.C. and D.H. Evans. 1972. Ion, water, and urea turnover rates in the nurse shark, *Ginglymostoma cirratum*. Comparative Biochemistry and Physiology 41A:761-764.

Carrier, J.C. and C.A. Luer. 1990. Growth rates in the nurse shark *Ginglymostoma cirratum*. COPEIA 1990(3):686-692.

Clark, E. 1959. Instrumental conditioning of lemon sharks. SCIENCE 130(3369):217-218.

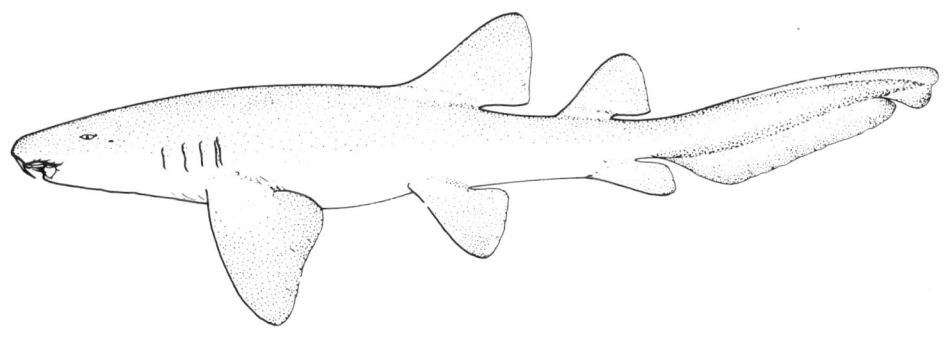

Nurse shark.

INSTRUMENTS OF NATURAL SELECTION:
How Important Are Sharks?

by WESLEY R. STRONG, JR.

The sun was falling quickly behind the parched hills of Catalina Island. For 20 minutes or so, the only detectable activity was the whispering of air through my snorkel. About 13 feet (four meters) below me, a juvenile horn shark, *Heterodontus francisci*, lay nestled against a rockpile. Nocturnal swimming activities are characteristic of these little sharks and were the subject of my research.

Suddenly, 10 or 12 jack mackerel, *Trachyurus symmetricus*, hurtled, tightly packed, toward the rocks I was watching. So close behind that it appeared somehow connected was a brown smoothhound shark, *Mustelus henlei*. Within centimeters of colliding with the rocks, the ball-shaped school obliterated, the fish disappearing in all directions. The shark braked to avoid crashing on the same rocks, a maneuver which cost it its dinner. It then turned, and cruised back into the darkness. The mackerel had made good their escape — this time.

When a mackerel is found in a shark's stomach, no one knows whether the fish was alive or dead when ingested. If it was alive, was it healthy? From nose to tail, blood cells to scales, was every bodily system intact and functioning at a level considered normal for the species? If it was healthy, was its behavior consistent with other mackerel? For example, did it exercise a proper schooling response? In short, why did the shark consume that particular mackerel?

These and many other questions directly relate to the predatory capabilities of the shark involved. I believe that these capabilities may be viewed as a continuum — *a predation-capacity continuum*. True scavengers would be located at the lower end, feeding solely on dead organisms. At the other extreme — the "super-predator," taking at will and regardless of an individual prey's fitness, any number of target species. In a pure sense, neither of these extremes serves to cull prey stocks; therefore, neither contributes to the evolution-driving process referred to as *natural selection* or *survival of the fittest*. It appears that the overwhelming majority of shark species, however, make their livings somewhere in between, performing "jobs" that require greater prey-catching abilities as they approach the super-predator end of the continuum.

Sharks that typically feed on diseased or wounded individuals would be one step higher than the scavengers. Higher yet, some sharks may select directly for or against genetically-encoded physical or behavioral traits such as coloration or escape responses. Approaching the super-predator level, sharks more capable of regularly capturing healthy prey may control populations and maintain prey species diversity by concentrating on the most available species.

Theoretically, sharks should exert the greatest selection pressure along the middle of the continuum, rather than at the ends. It should be noted that many species shift their positions, switching predatory modes as they develop or as prey opportunities arise on a seasonal or even daily basis. Until we understand where various sharks primarily occur on this continuum, we cannot assess their effectiveness as instruments of their preys' evolution.

When diving with mako sharks, *Isurus*

Strong, a researcher for the Cousteau Society, is currently investigating Australia's white sharks. He is also a doctoral candidate at the University of California, Santa Barbara, and his dissertation research is part of the University of Miami's lemon shark project.

oxyrinchus, you can see how their effortless glides occasionally erupt into bursts of speed that plainly challenge the capabilities of other pelagic fishes. It is interesting that bonitos have been found whole, without so much as teeth-marks, in makos' stomachs. This implies that relatively healthy prey were swallowed "in flight." But while stomach contents and scars are useful in deducing predator/prey interactions, they do not provide all the information essential for identifying the predator's true role in the ecosystem.

Attacks generally happen fast, as in the failed attempt described earlier. Sharks typically swim at relatively slow "cruising" speeds, conserving energy and reducing the likelihood of alerting potential prey; speed bursts are saved for escape and feeding. Compared to similar-sized bony fishes, sharks do not require large amounts of food and probably do not eat as often. Add to these facts the concealing nature of the sharks' environment, and it is easy to understand our ignorance of their predatory behaviors. Slowly, though, we are filling in the gaps with direct observations of shark predation.

Some observations are possible because they happen on the sea surface. Last summer, at French Frigate Shoals in the Northwest Hawaiian Islands, I observed 138 attacks by tiger sharks, *Galeocerdo cuvieri*, on fledgling albatrosses. The young albatrosses routinely alighted on the water following their first, short flights from shore. Tiger sharks cruised the lagoon and, on encountering one of the birds, dashed the final meter or two in an attempt to intercept it at the surface. Half of the observed attacks were successful. The first flight of a young bird is but a flicker in its life history, yet sharks killed nearly 10% of those observed leaving their small rookery. Researchers at Southeast Farallon Island recently reported 81 attacks by white sharks, *Carcharodon carcharias*, on pin-

Great hammerhead shark with carcass of captured southern stingray and attendant shark-suckers lower right. Photo by W. R. Strong.

nipeds. In both cases, work continues but these remarkable incidences of predation clearly exert some control over pinniped and albatross numbers and potentially select for their intelligence, agility, and other survival-related attributes.

Another study found that elephant seals, *Mirounga angustirostris*, bearing fresh shark-bite wounds had significantly lower reproductive success than their immediate neighbors. Therefore, if an elephant seal is bitten because it is physically or mentally less capable of detecting or avoiding a shark, then even if it survives, it is less likely to reproduce. Resources are thereby left for the offspring of "fitter" seals.

Underwater observations of shark predation are less common, but they do happen. In the Bahamas, on 24 May 1988, I observed an incredible series of events including the pursuit, attack, and consumption of a southern stingray, *Dasyatis americana*, by a great hammerhead shark, *Sphyrna mokarran*. The hammerhead outswam, adeptly dispatched, then leisurely ate the ray. The slain ray had appeared healthy, but wandered farther from the protective cover of a nearby shipwreck than other rays that were not attacked. It is interesting that, later in the same episode, blacktip, *Carcharhinus limbatus*, and sharpnose sharks, *Rhizoprionodon terraenovae*, responded as scavengers, feeding on bits of the ray's carcass.

A candidate for the super-predator title is, strangely enough, the angel shark, *Squatina californica*. This awkward-looking shark strikes from the sea floor, engulfing fish, squid, and virtually any small organism that happens to swim near its mouth. Because of their style of ambush predation, angel sharks consume a variety of unsuspecting, but nevertheless healthy prey.

How important are sharks in helping to shape the marine ecosystems of tomorrow? Obviously, we still don't know. Predation accounts for only one of the many external biological and environ-

Tiger shark attacking posterior of blackfooted albatross as other albatrosses stand by on shore. This bird survived. Photo by W. R. Strong.

mental factors exerting, on prey, the pressure to evolve. Nonetheless, predation plays a role, and a growing body of evidence indicates that many sharks are active, aggressive predators. Furthermore, it is generally accepted that steady selection exerted by environmental pressure leads to ecological diversity and stability. If we agree that these are good things, sound management of sharks and other apex predators is needed, at least until we better understand some of the subtleties surrounding the fitness and acquisition of their various prey. The Nature Conservancy has a wonderful slogan, "Intelligent tinkerers save all the pieces."

ADDITIONAL READING:

Ainley, D.G., C.S. Strong, H.R. Huber, T.J. Lewis, S.H. Morrell. 1981. Predation by sharks on pinnipeds at the Farallon Islands. Fishery Bulletin. 78(4):941-945.

Strong, W.R., F.F. Snelson, and S.H. Gruber. 1990. Hammerhead shark predation on stingrays: an observation of prey handling by *Sphyrna mokarran*. Copeia 1990(3):836-840.

Seven-foot tiger shark, Hawaii. Photo by W. R. Strong.

Feeding Biology of Sharks

by BRAD WETHERBEE

Sharks are among the best known but least understood predators in the sea and are often thought of as voracious eaters, consuming anything they encounter. Many people are impressed by the way sharks capture and devour their prey, and some people are frightened of sharks because they are one of the few remaining animals capable of killing and eating humans. Curious items (license plates for instance) reportedly found in the stomachs of sharks have also sparked some interest in the feeding habits of these animals. Some fishermen despise sharks because they compete for fish, damage fishing gear, and destroy fish left in nets or on lines. Large numbers of sharks are common in marine environments, and they may eat many fish and other marine animals. Consequently, scientists are interested in the impact that sharks have on the animals in a particular area. For all of these reasons there is interest in what sharks eat and how they go about capturing their food.

What Sharks Eat

Examination of shark stomachs has shown that for most species, about 70 - 80% of the diet consists of bony fishes. Different species of shark eat different species of bony fishes, but the percentage of bony fish eaten remains high. Most sharks also eat a small percentage of invertebrates such as octopus, crabs, or other shellfish. Again, the types of invertebrates eaten vary, but the percentage is generally low. However, the leopard shark, *Triakis semifasciata*, and a few other species eat a much smaller quantity of fish. Their diets are made up almost entirely of invertebrates.

Some sharks, such as the white, tiger, and cookie cutter, are somewhat specialized for feeding regularly on marine mammals. While these sharks are capable of feeding on live seals, sea lions, sea otters, dolphins, or whales, the majority of sharks eat marine mammals only when they come upon a dead one. Cannibalism is common, and many sharks eat rays or other types of sharks, as well as members of their own species. Hammerhead sharks are thought to take advantage of the sensory capabilities of their broad-shaped heads to detect rays buried in the sand. Galapagos, tiger, and bull sharks are other well known cannibalistic sharks.

The two largest species, the whale shark, *Rhincodon typus*, which reportedly reaches lengths near 60 feet, and the basking shark, *Cetorhinus maximus*, which may grow to over 40 feet, have an unusual feeding method. These two species, along with the recently discovered megamouth shark, *Megachasma pelagios*, are specially adapted for filtering small organisms out of the water. Using their gill rakers to filter tremendous quantities of water, they consume large numbers of small fish, crustaceans, or other planktonic invertebrates, in a method similar to the filter feeding of baleen whales.

Although the diet of sharks is tremendously varied, not everything eaten is digestible. Mud, stones, and plants found in the stomachs of sharks are thought to have been ingested along with food taken off the bottom of the ocean. The list of strange articles supposedly found in the stomachs of sharks includes a suit of armor, a barrel of nails, a roll of tar paper, bottles, cans, coal, raincoats, shoes, belts, plastic bags, goats, horses, sheep, lizards, snakes, chickens, reindeer, and monkeys. Most of these land animals are not actually hunted by sharks, but have drowned or were discarded into the sea by humans. Such items are rarely found

A doctoral candidate in zoology at the University of Hawaii, Wetherbee is studying deep-sea shark buoyancy in relation to the ecology of sharks.

in the stomachs of most sharks, but there are a few species (tiger and bull sharks for example) which have extremely varied diets and may swallow unusual objects more frequently than other species.

Several theories explain the occurrence of these objects. Sharks may simply swallow indigestible items accidentally along with food, or when they are investigating an object as a potential meal.

location to the next, and as they grow larger. Sharks are opportunistic feeders, which means they are able to utilize diverse food sources depending on the availability of each food type. Many juvenile sharks spend the early portions of their lives in bays or estuaries which serve as nursery grounds. Here, the sharks may have a somewhat limited diet due to the scarcity of food in these

Tiger shark preying upon a blackfooted albatross, French Frigate Shoals, Northwest Hawaiian Islands. Photo by T. M. Moser.

They may also be attracted to and swallow metal objects because of their ability to detect electrical fields produced by the objects. Another theory is that heavy items are swallowed intentionally for ballast so that sharks can control their buoyancy, much like a submarine takes on ballast to shift position in the water column. When sharks are caught they sometimes evert their stomachs. Aquarium workers have observed captive sharks evert their stomachs, yet continue to swim and behave normally. The stomachs of most of the captive sharks are eventually returned to the interior of their bodies, and the sharks remain in good health. This ability to evert their stomachs possibly provides a means for sharks to empty their stomachs of indigestible objects.

Feeding Habits of Sharks

There is considerable variation in the diet of many sharks from one season or

restricted habitats. Diversity of prey is thus sacrificed for safety from predators such as larger sharks. As they grow older the young sharks move offshore and encounter more and more types of food, and the diversity of their diet increases.

Some sharks take advantage of seasonal migrations or runs of fish, feeding almost exclusively on large schools of fish or squid at certain times of the year. When the schools are no longer present the sharks must shift to another food source or rely on an array of food items rather than a single item. For example, mako sharks, *Isurus oxyrinchus,* of the northwest Atlantic feed extensively on bluefish during winter and spring, but they eat more squid in the summer when the bluefish have migrated inshore. As a shark moves from one location to another, it is bound to encounter differing levels of abundance of prey in each new area. Versatile food habits are advantageous to the individual shark because feeding will not be limited to a particular prey throughout the year. This may allow sharks to increase population density, decrease competition between individuals, and to broaden their range and distribution.

One unusual aspect of feeding is cooperative hunting which has been reported in a number of species. The sharks work together in varying degrees to herd and feed upon schools of fish. In one such instance reef blacktip sharks, *Carcharhinus melanopterus,* drove fish into shallow water and onto the shore. Then the sharks wriggled on shore to feed on the stranded fish.

Many people think that sharks live a life of perpetual ambush, pursuit, and attack and are always actively engaged in the search for food. This view has changed recently, as an increasing amount of information is gathered about the feeding habits of sharks. There are several pieces of evidence indicating that sharks feed intensively for a short time and then feed very little for a longer period of time. First of all, a large percentage of captured sharks have empty stomachs or have well digested prey in their stomachs. Considering that food is eliminated from the stomachs of sharks at a rate slower than many animals, a shark with an empty stomach had probably eaten its last meal at least 24 hours before it was captured.

There are also many reports of sharks with full stomachs being caught. Even though these sharks had just eaten, they were still attracted to bait (some attacked the bait violently) and were still willing to consume more food. The number of different food items found in the stomach is usually low, indicating that sharks generally do not consume additional prey after they have already eaten. These findings suggest that there is a short period of feeding activity when sharks are in a feeding mode, followed by a longer period of digestion when feeding is minimal. Researchers estimate that the average lemon shark, *Negaprion brevirostris,* feeds actively for about 11 hours and then fasts for the next 32 hours.

Rate of consumption has been estimated for a number of species of sharks based primarily on the amount of food found in their stomachs. In each case, sharks were found to consume very little when compared to most bony fish and many other animals. While it appears that sharks can consume the equivalent of their body weight in about one month, many carnivorous bony fish eat an equivalent of their body weight in a few days. Contrary to the notion that sharks are continuously eating, they actually consume a proportionately small amount of food and may often pass up potential prey because they are not inclined to feed for relatively long periods of time.

As we learn more about feeding in sharks it will be clearer to what degree sharks are discriminating feeders, and why they may pass up one type of food and eat another. Knowledge of the types and amount of food consumed by sharks will be useful in assessing their impact on marine environments and their role in transferring energy within ecosystems. Because our reliance on resources from the sea will continue to increase, it will be more important to understand the level of competition between man and sharks for these limited resources.

ADDITIONAL READING:

Cortes, E. and S.H. Gruber, 1990. Diet, feeding habits and estimates of daily ration of young lemon sharks, *Negaprion brevirostris.* Copeia 1990 (1):204-218.

Lyle, J.M. 1983. Food and feeding habits of the lesser spotted dogfish, *Scyliorhinus canicula* (L.), in Isle of Man Waters. Journal of Fish Biology 23:725-737.

Medved, R.J. and J.A. Marshall. 1981. Feeding behavior and biology of young sandbar sharks, *Carcharhinus plumbeus* (Pices, Carcharhinidae), in Chincoteague Bay, Virginia. Fisheries Bulletin 79(3):441-447.

Tricas, T.C. 1979. Relationships of the blue shark, *Prionace glauca,* and its prey species near Santa Catalina Island, California. Fisheries Bulletin 77(1):175-182.

The Ravenous Mako

by CHUCK STILLWELL

Not much is known about the rate of food consumption and the impact of most shark species on their prey groups. Evidence does show, however, that food consumption is related to the rate at which food is digested and the activity level of a particular species. Sedentary and slow-moving species such as the nurse shark, *Ginglymostoma cirratum,* may eat 0.2-0.3 percent of its body weight per day and take at least six days to digest an average-sized meal. More active species such as the sandbar, *Carcharhinus plumbeus,* and blue shark, *Prionace glauca,* consume 0.2-0.6 percent of their body weight per day, but digest an average meal in 3-4 days. One of the most active species, the mako shark, *Isurus oxyrinchus,* will eat 3 percent of its body weight per day and digest an average-sized meal in 1.5-2.0 days.

In general, mako food consumption amounts to an average of 4 pounds per day (called the "daily ration"), or an equivalent of just over 10 times the average body weight (139 pounds) per year. To compensate for energy expended during periods of active metabolism (prey search, attack, migration), the resulting daily ration could approach 5.5 pounds per day, increasing the annual consumption to possibly 12-15 times the average body weight. The large amount of food required by the mako is not only for physiological maintenance and movement, but also to accommodate a very rapid growth rate.

A growth study of this species shows that following a birth weight of 5-6 pounds, males grow to around 300 pounds in 4.5-5.0 years, while females reach approximately 500 pounds by age 7. In the first three years of life, the weight may increase an average of 60 pounds per year. In contrast to the mako, the sandbar shark, a relatively large (200 + pounds, maximum size) inshore species, will consume approximately one-quarter pound of food per day and take 12-14 years to attain a weight of 90-100 pounds.

To provide the metabolic energy required by the mako to live its fast-paced life, the food consumed must be digested and processed at an accelerated rate. This is accomplished by an elevated body temperature, 12-18 degrees F. above ambient (most fish have body temperatures equal to that of the water), and a controllable blood network that can direct warmed blood to the stomach and intestines, thereby increasing the rate of digestion. The white, *Carcharodon carcharias,* and porbeagle sharks, *Lamna nasus,* relatives of the mako, share similar heat-retaining systems. Because of their streamlined and warm bodies, it is suggested that makos' metabolic capacities may rival those of some highly evolved teleosts, such as the tunas.

The primary food of the mako consists of various fish species occurring throughout the water column, from bottom-dwelling eelpout and searobins, to pelagic tunas and swordfish. A shift to large prey, such as swordfish, appears to occur when makos attain weights greater than 300 pounds. Accounts of makos attacking and eating large swordfish of 400 pounds or more are not uncommon. Although bony fish comprise almost 70% of the mako's diet, squid contributes about 15% overall, and are eaten most frequently offshore where depths are greater than 600 feet.

Off the northeast coast of the United States, bluefish are the mako's most important food. National Marine Fisheries Service biologists examined hundreds of stomachs in this area and found that

A fisheries biologist with NMFS, Narragansett, RI, Stillwell has studied sharks for 25 years with an emphasis on their food habits.

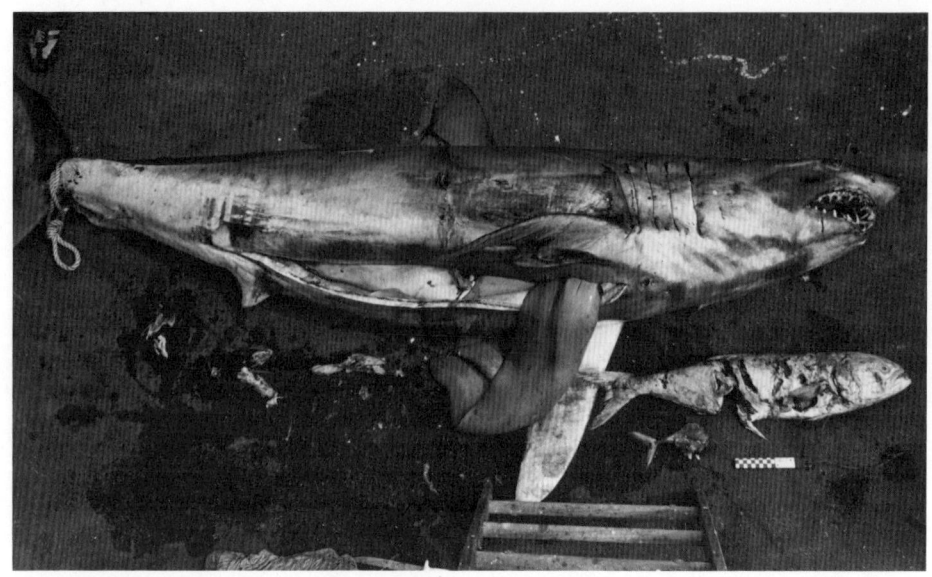

A 518-pound female mako shark with a 14-pound bluefish removed from its stomach. Photo by H.W. Pratt.

bluefish comprise 77% of the mako's food by volume, and that 400+ pound makos have the speed and agility to pursue, seize, and swallow 12-15 pound bluefish whole or in two to three pieces. The biomass of bluefish consumed by the mako population in the area from Cape Hatteras, NC, to Georges Bank off southern New England, is estimated to be 8,500 tons or 7.3% of the bluefish in this region.

The mako population along the U.S. Atlantic coast has been relatively stable over the past 15 years and may be tied to a continual abundance of bluefish. If this predator-prey relationship should collapse because of a decline in bluefish availability, we may witness a serious reduction in a premier fish species, the mako shark.

ADDITIONAL READING:

Ellis, R. 1975. THE BOOK OF SHARKS. Grosset and Dunlop.

McCormick, H.W., T. Allen, W.E. Young. SHADOWS IN THE SEA. Weathervane Books.

Moss, S.A. 1984. SHARKS: AN INTRODUCTION FOR THE AMATEUR NATURALIST. Prentice Hall.

Springer, V.C. and J.P. Gold. 1989. SHARKS IN QUESTION.

Mako Shark

How Deep Do Sharks Go?
Reflections on Deep Sea Sharks
by EUGENIE CLARK and EMORY KRISTOF

Living marine creatures, from bacteria to fish, inhabit the deepest parts of the ocean. A sole and shrimp were seen from the bathyscaphe *Trieste* during the record 35,800 feet (7 miles) dive in the Challenger Deep off Guam in 1960. Sharks are certainly among the largest, most imposing creatures of the deep sea, but they don't seem to go as deep as bony fishes or their relatives the skates and chimeras. We found no evidence that they go much deeper than 12,000 feet.

The deepest accurate record of a living shark was made by John Issacs with a robot camera set down along with a can of bait at 6,300 feet off Baja California. The resulting photograph revealed the head of a large Pacific sleeper shark, *Somniosus pacificus*. Its length, compared to the visible, 13-inch diameter bait can, must have been at least 12 feet. During a recent series of submersible dives in Suruga Bay, Japan, the largest shark known in the deep sea was filmed at 4,000 feet, and turned out to be a female Pacific sleeper shark that we estimated to be more than 23 feet long (Doubilet et al. 1990).

The Portuguese shark, *Centroscymnus coelolepis*, seems to hold the record for going deeper than any species of shark. In 1984 Compagno reported that this shark has a depth range of 900 to 12,000 feet and is caught commercially with deep water bottom trawls, nets, and lines. It is commonly caught in gear set at 1,300 feet. There is a possibility, however, that some of these records are derived from commercial fishing operations that may catch some sharks when the gear is on the way up or down.

During the past four years (1987 to 1990) we have conducted 71 dives in seven deep-diving manned submersibles as part of the Beebe Project which was named after William Beebe, the first biologist to explore the deep sea in the bathysphere and describe the animals he saw (Beebe 1934). Begun in Bermuda in 1987, our on-going project has been supported continuously by the National Geographic Society, through the programs of Emory Kristof, and by various governmental agencies, private companies and individuals, and academic institutions.

In these dives we lured deep sea sharks with bait to observe and photograph them in their natural habitat (Kristof and Chandler 1987). With the submersible settled on the bottom during dives of 1,000 to 12,000 feet, we set out bait and waited. The long (up to 17 1/2 hours), quiet dives and baiting technique have been successful in bringing in as many as 21 individual sharks in one dive. Our dive sites have been located off the coast of Bermuda, Bahamas, Grand Cayman, California's Monterey Canyon, Japan's Suruga Bay, and near the Chiagos Archipelago in the Indian Ocean. Through an international effort, we have made dives down as far as 12,000 feet in the U.S. *Alvin*, the Soviet *Mir I & II*, the French *Nautile*, and the Canadian-made *Pisces II* and *VI*. For shallower dives of 980 to 1,200 feet we used the PC 1802 and the Johnson Sea Link.

One of the surprising observations and data we gathered from sub dives was the prevalence of a "pineal window" (Gruber et al. 1975) in three types of sharks. The "window" is a relatively

Clark, a zoology professor at the University of Maryland, is an American Littoral Society vice president and a frequent contributor to its publications. Kristof, a National Geographic staff photographer, specializes in deep water photography using cameras both remotely operated and mounted on submersibles.

SHARKS OBSERVED FROM BAITED SUBMERSIBLES 1986-1990
BEEBE PROJECT

SHARKS	NUMBER SEEN	LOCATIONS	DEPTHS OBSERVED meters	PINEAL EYE
1. Hexanchus griseus SIXGILL SHARK	78/94	Grand Cayman & Bermuda	300-1560	X
2. Hexanchus vitulus BIGEYE SIXGILL	10	Grand Cayman, Bermuda & Bahamas	297-711	-
3. Centrophorus 4 Species GULPER SHARKS	75/97	Grand Cayman, Bermuda, Bahamas & Japan	520-978	X
4. Centroscymnus 2 Species mainly PORTUGUESE DOGFISH	19	Bermuda, Japan & Indian Ocean	900-1640-1930	-
5. Dalatias licha KITEFIN SHARK	3	Grand Cayman & Bermuda	914-1645	-
6. Etmopterus 3 Species LANTERN SHARKS	13+	Bermuda & Japan	350-920	X
7. Somniosus pacificus PACIFIC SLEEPER SHARK	3	California, Japan & Indian Ocean	900-1562-1630	-
8. Mustelus GUMMY SHARK	14/17	Grand Cayman, Bermuda & Bahamas	297-752	-
9. Galeocerdo cuvieri TIGER SHARK	1	Grand Cayman	305	-
10. Isurus paucus LONGFIN MAKO	1	Grand Cayman	748	-
11. Apristiurus deep water CATSHARK	6	Grand Cayman, Bermuda	876-1150	-
12. Cephaloscyllium isabellum SWELLSHARK	2	Japan	350	-
13. Pseudotriakis microdon FALSE CATSHARK	1	Japan	580	-
TOTAL	225/266			

Immature female sixgill shark, Hexanchus griseus, about nine feet long attracted to bait cage deployed from manipulator arm of Pisces VI submersible (in background) photographed by remote control, depth about 2,000 ft., Bermuda. Photo by E. Kristof.

PC 1802 just under the surface with Drs. Sol Klotz and E. Clark, observers at the large acrylic "bubble window," at the start of a dive to 1,000 ft., Grand Cayman, 1987. Photo by E. Kristof.

DEPTH RANGES OF DEEPSEA SHARKS IN RELATION TO SUNLIGHT PENETRATION

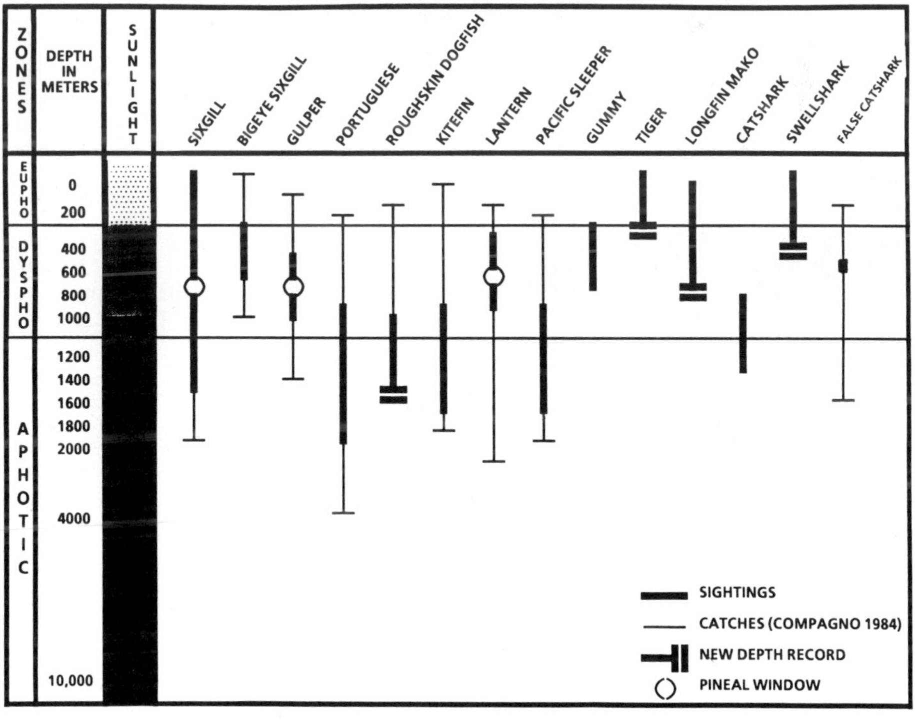

- ■ SIGHTINGS
- | CATCHES (COMPAGNO 1984)
- ⊣|⊢ NEW DEPTH RECORD
- ○ PINEAL WINDOW

Mature sixgill male, Hexanchus griseus, about 11.5 ft. TL at 1,000 ft. photographed from the PC 1802 submersible, Grand Cayman. The bait also attracted hundreds of shrimp and a crab seen in the background. Photo by E. Clark.

transparent patch of skin over the pineal gland located on the top of a shark's head. The largest species of the sixgill sharks, *Hexanchus griseus*, gulper sharks of the genus *Centrophorus*, and lantern sharks of the genus *Etmopterus*, as reported in more detail by Clark & Kristof (1990), had obvious pineal windows. These sharks show depth ranges that extend from the euphotic to the aphotic zones and are most common in the dysphotic zone. Sharks probably use the underlying pineal gland as a light receiving organ to detect downwelling light. Such a function has been postulated for a myctophid (lantern) fish and a squid (Young et al. 1979) as a means for sensing the amount of sunlight penetration. The pineal complex may aid these deep-sea sharks in their search for food. The pineal window is absent in the bigeye sixgill shark, *Hexanchus vitulus*, that inhabits only the euphotic and dysphotic zones and has bigger eyes.

The Beebe Project's submersible dives established four new depth-related records: three for shallow water sharks such as the tiger shark and one for the deep-sea roughskin dogfish. Our four deepest dives were between 6,800 and 12,000 feet. We saw no sharks, but many deep-sea bony fishes and other cartilagenous fishes (skates and chimeras) were attracted to our bait. Yet, in the same geographic area, but in shallower (1,000 to 6,000 feet) water, many sharks were attracted to our baited submersibles. Such negative results at greater depths suggest to us that sharks may not normally inhabit water deeper than 7,000 feet, and may never be abundant there. However, we plan to continue our search for deep sea sharks in an effort to reveal the diversity and complexity of the shark fauna and their true depth ranges.

* * *

NOTE: Results given in this short essay are summarized from our previous reports published mainly in National Geographic magazine and reflect the ef-

Centrophorus uyato, about 31 inches long, depth 2,600 ft., Grand Cayman. Note the pineal "window." Photo by E. Kristof.

Female tiger shark, Galeocerdo cuvieri, about 8.5 ft. long, photographed at Grand Cayman, depth 1,000 ft., a record. Photo by E. Kristof.

Deep water gummy shark, Mustelus sp., about 28 inches long, Grand Cayman. Photo by J.I. Castro.

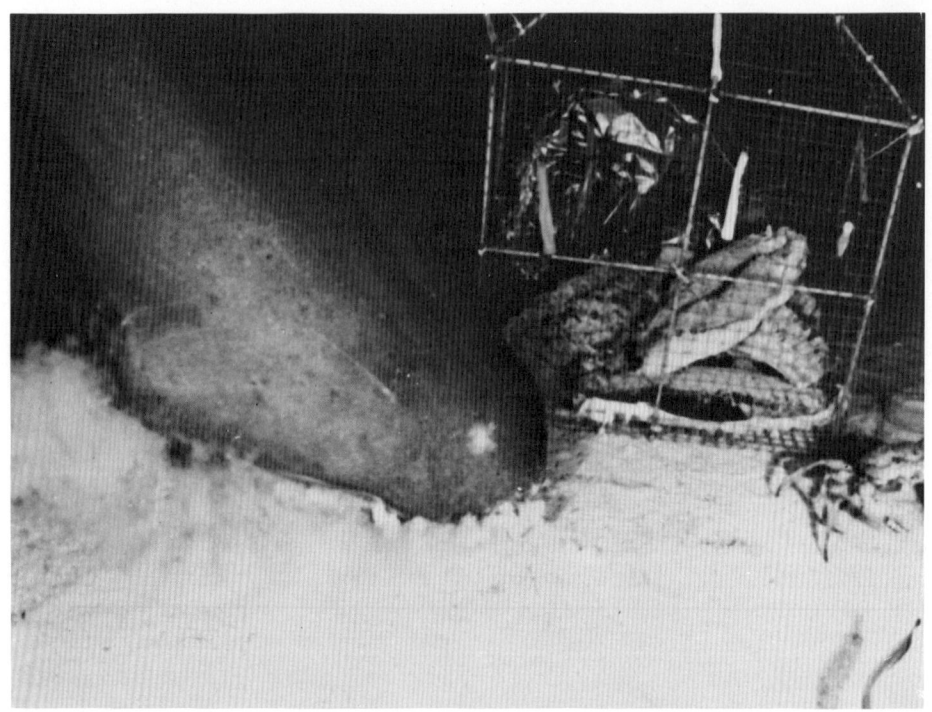

Adult male sixgill shark, Hexanchus griseus, mouthing the sand in front of bait cage, Bermuda. The light spot on top of the head is the pineal "window." Photo by E. Kristof.

forts of many teams of marine scientists and photographers.

ACKNOWLEDGEMENT: The senior author wishes to thank Stewart Springer for his help in her studies of sharks over the decades. When we discovered that the sleeping sharks in Mexican caves were very clever and clean, and named the species after Stew, *Carcharhinus springeri*, he was pleased to learn of the habits of his namesake. Unfortunately, the name *C. perezi* turned out to have priority, but Stewart Springer's name will stand forever as one of the greatest in the annals of shark studies. I don't mind that Stew's marvelous monograph on catsharks in 1979 meant that my first scientific paper on sharks in 1947, had the wrong scientific name in its title! I feel honored to be the first to see alive his deep-sea bigeye sixgill shark, *Hexabranchus vitulus*, swimming in its natural habitat. It was named from dead specimens by Stew and Waller who recognized it was a distinct species and not the young of *H. griseus*. Many thanks to Stew for his meticulous and valuable contributions to ichthyology.

ADDITIONAL READING:

Beebe, W. 1934. A half mile down. Nat. Geogr. 66(6):661-704.

Clark, E. and E. Kristof. 1990. Deep sea elasmobranchs observed from submersibles in Grand Cayman, Bermuda and Bahamas. *In*: Elasmobranchs as Living Resources NOAA Tech. Rep. 90:275-290.

Doubilet, D., E. Kristof and E. Clark. 1990. Suruga Bay, in the shadow of Mt. Fuji. Nat. Geogr. 178(4):2-39.

Gruber, S.H., D.J. Hamasaki and B.L. Davis. 1975. Window to the epiphysis in sharks. Copeia. (2):378-380.

Kristof, E. and A. Chandler. 1987. Using Pisces VI as a deep sea blind. Mar. Tech Soc. Proc. ROV-87 Conference: 225-227.

Young, R.E., C.F.E. Roper and J.F. Walters. 1979. Eyes and extraocular photoreceptors in mid-water cephalopods and fishes: their roles in detecting downwelling light for counterillumination. Mar. Biol. 51:371-380.

Home Range of Juvenile Lemon Sharks

by JOHN F. MORRISSEY

For many years the daily movements and activity patterns of all shark species were a complete mystery. Sharks live in a concealing medium, so sustained, direct, visual observation is impossible in all but a few rare instances. Established techniques used to study the movement patterns of terrestrial animals are useless for aquatic species. Shark tagging projects have provided information only on the long-term movements of sharks.

shark, *Negaprion brevirostris*, of the Bahamas. More than 20 juvenile lemon sharks in the North Sound of Bimini, Bahamas, were fitted with internal ultrasonic transmitters and tracked for periods ranging from 12-39 days. Slowly, an understanding of the movements of these young sharks is being obtained.

Juvenile lemon sharks (2-2.5 ft. long) typically occupy an area of the sand flats close to shore in water less than three feet

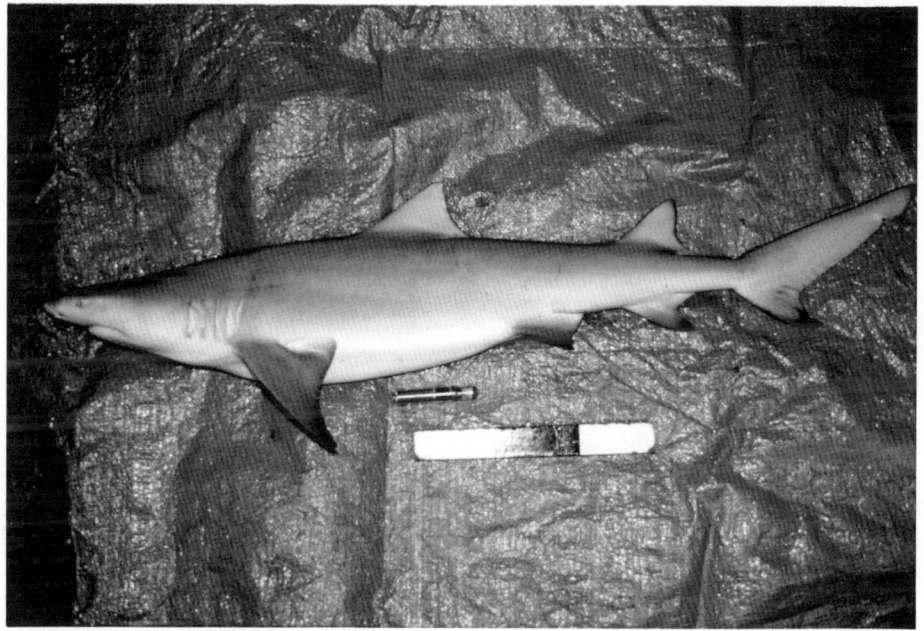

A lemon shark with an acoustic transmitter. Photo by J. Morrissey.

Recently, however, the technique of acoustic telemetry has enabled researchers to investigate the activity of many aquatic species, including sharks. In terms of activity one of the most intensively studied shark species is the lemon

Morrissey is a NMFS fishery biologist and a doctoral candidate at the University of Miami's Rosenstiel School of Marine and Atmospheric Science. His dissertation research is on activity patterns of lemon sharks in the Bahamas.

deep. Their daily activity consists of long slow laps along the mangrove-fringed shoreline. This repeated behavior over the same location allows scientists to refer appropriately to the activity spaces of juvenile lemon sharks as home ranges. An analysis of habitat selection has shown that young lemon sharks, perhaps as a strategy to avoid predators (e.g., larger sharks), prefer shallow water, and are usually found along the shoreline.

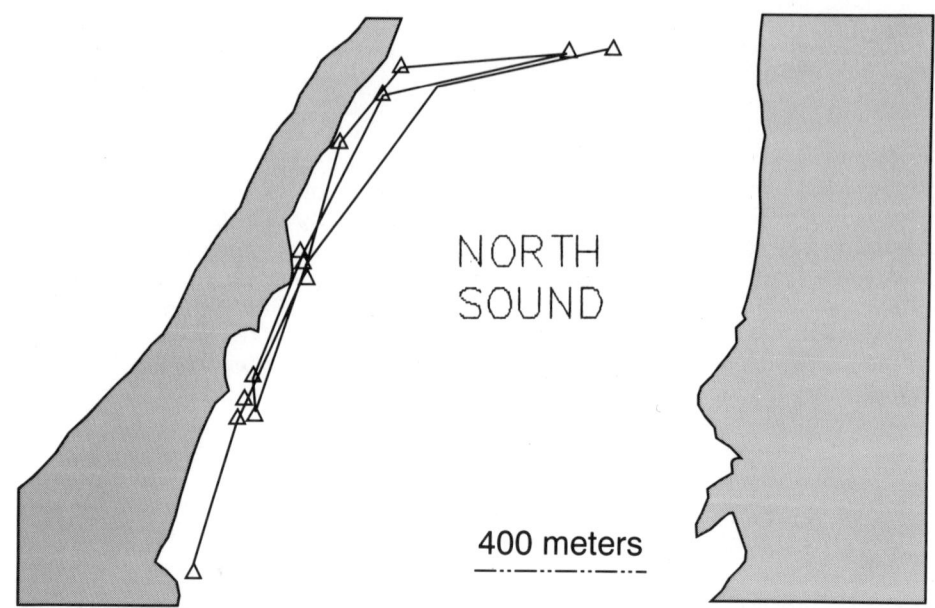

A partial track of shark "Moe,", August 5, 1989, between 6:15pm and 9:15 pm. These 15-minute fixes exemplify typical movement patterns of juvenile lemon sharks — repeated laps along shoreline with occasional excursions into deeper water.

However, if the water depth remains shallow, they frequently will range hundreds of meters from shore.

While young lemon sharks are quite site-attached, they have not been observed defending their home ranges. The home ranges of neighboring sharks overlap broadly, and neighboring sharks have even been observed in cooperative feeding behavior. Several sharks will herd a school of baitfish against the shore and then alternately dive into the school for a mouthful. Therefore, lemon sharks, like all other shark species studied to date, are not territorial. The assumption that a shark is defending its territory when attacking a human is not supported by telemetry data.

The home range of the juvenile lemon shark averages about 150 acres or 0.69 km^2, and the area increases as the shark ages. The home range of one 70-inch (180 cm) lemon shark was estimated to be about seven square miles or 18 km^2, and that of a 90-inch (230 cm) individual to be 36 square miles or 93 km^2. During the individual's lifetime the location of the home range changes also, moving after several years from the shallow nursery area, to the open sand flats, and ultimately to the reefs and beyond.

The speed of these young sharks averages about 0.27 body lengths per second, but varies greatly. At times they will spend several hours lying on the sand among the prop roots of red mangrove trees. Then they burst to speeds of greater than one body length per second. This variation results in a crepuscular activity pattern where young lemon sharks patrol during dawn and dusk at speeds twice those maintained during day and night.

Future study and analysis will produce a more complete understanding of movement patterns during all life history stages for lemon sharks in the Caribbean Sea.

Long Distance Movements of Atlantic Sharks
FROM THE NMFS COOPERATIVE SHARK TAGGING PROGRAM

by J.G. CASEY and N.E. KOHLER

In 1962 the U.S. Government initiated a shark tagging program in the Atlantic Ocean with the volunteer assistance of sport and commercial fishermen. From 1962 through 1966 the study, directed by J.G. Casey, was centered at the Sandy Hook (NJ) Marine Laboratory within the U.S. Fish and Wildlife Service of the Department of the Interior. Since 1966, the program has been conducted from NOAA's National Marine Fisheries Service Laboratory in Narragansett, RI. A detailed account of the program's early history and summary of results for the period 1962 through 1982 are provided in an earlier publication (Casey, 1985).

Currently, the Cooperative Shark Tagging Program involves about 4,000 recreational anglers, commercial fishermen, scientists, and Foreign Fisheries Observers distributed along the Atlantic and Gulf coasts from Maine to Texas and from the Canary Islands, England, Mexico, Spain, Portugal, Poland, Italy, and the Bahamas. Over the years, the number of sharks tagged annually has varied from 100 in the early years to an average of about 5,000 per year in the past five years. In recent years, sportsmen have tagged about 50% of the sharks, followed by NMFS and other biologists (22%), U.S. Foreign Fisheries Observers aboard Japanese tuna boats (20%), and commercial fishermen (8%). Up to the present, over 87,000 fish representing 46 species of sharks and 20 species of other fishes have been tagged. Of these, over 3,200 fish from 32 species of sharks have been recaptured (a recapture rate of approximately 4%). Recaptures have been returned by fishermen from 24 countries and island territories. This shark tagging program is the largest conducted anywhere in the world. It owes its success to the thousands of fishermen who have unselfishly assisted in the tagging effort and in providing valuable data from log books, tournament records, and observations of sharks at sea.

Fish tagging can have several objectives, including studies of migrations, age, rates of growth, identification of different stocks, and population dynamics (e.g., assessing the size of the population, the size and age of individuals making up the populations, whether the population is increasing, decreasing, or remaining stable). Tagging data also provide information for monitoring shark populations that can help detect changes in species composition, geographical distributions, and size compositions. These variables can then be compared to shifts in prey abundance or environmental changes such as annual rainfall, water temperature, or the effects of fishing, pollution, and other man-made influences.

In addition to the scientific interest and the practical applications of tagging information to immediate management initiatives, there are also discoveries that gain the attention of a broad segment of society simply because they are "interesting." Questions commonly asked include: How many sharks have been tagged? How fast do they swim? What is the longest time at liberty? How long does a shark live? How far do they travel? One problem with attempting to answer questions about "sharks" is that there are an estimated 350 species in the world, and they are so different in many respects that very few answers can be applied to

Casey is the chief of the Apex Predators Investigation (API) of the National Marine Fisheries Service Laboratory, Narragansett, RI. Kohler works on shark life history studies in API at the same lab.

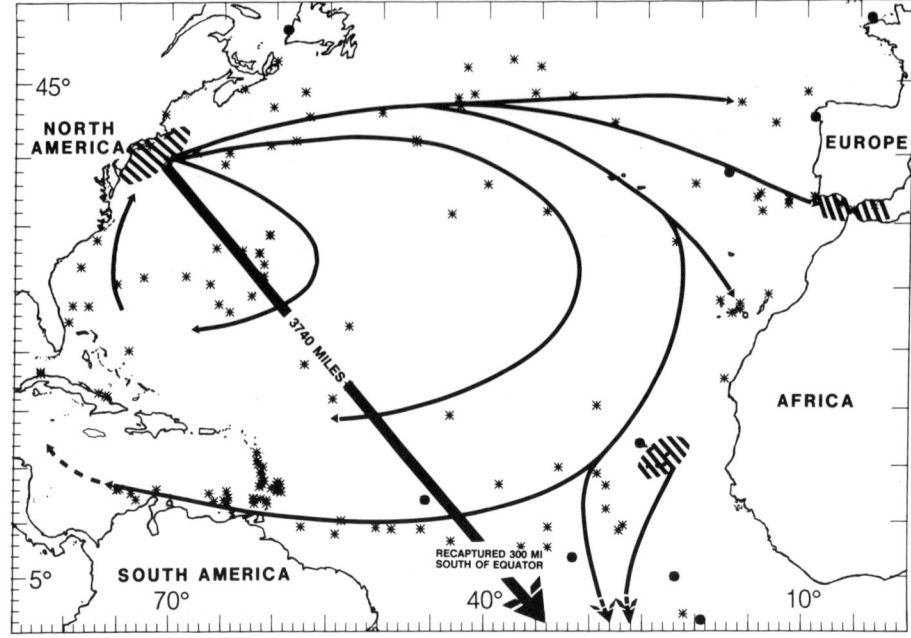
Blue shark tag returns from the North Atlantic Ocean (greater than 500 miles).

all sharks. Accordingly, the rest of this article is offered in answer to the question, "How far have tagged sharks travelled?"

For the sake of convenience, the sharks considered here can be categorized as: (1) highly pelagic (those that range over broad geographical areas, sometimes occupying entire ocean basins), (2) coastal pelagic (those that are generally confined to the continental shelves but have shown movements exceeding 1,000 miles), and (3) local or resident (those that apparently spend most of their lives in a limited range of a few hundred miles or less). Bull, nurse, and bonnethead sharks are examples of local species. Although we are not considering the movements of these and other local species in this article, we hasten to point out that populations of local elasmobranchs are highly important components of marine ecosystems. Moreover, they are the most vulnerable to the impact of human activities, including habitat degradation and intensive fishing.

Of the 32 shark species from which tags were recovered under the NMFS program, 10 species have demonstrated movements exceeding 1,000 miles between tag and recapture locations. The distances in miles are calculated as straight-line distances. With the exception of the oceanic whitetip shark, the maximum distance for each species is supported by additional, if somewhat shorter, long-range tag returns. For example, the averages of the five farthest distances traveled for the shark species shown in the figures are as follows: blue (3,383 mi.), sandbar (1,994 mi.), dusky (1,888 mi.), mako (1,909 mi.), tiger (1,351 mi.), bignose (1,202 mi.), night (908 mi.), blacktip (771 mi.), and bigeye thresher sharks (745 mi.).

These maximum distances between tag and recapture locations are measured as straight lines and do not reflect random movements, or the effects of current systems, temperature zones, and other environmental features that influence migratory pathways and would certainly increase these distances significantly. For example the maximum straight-line dis-

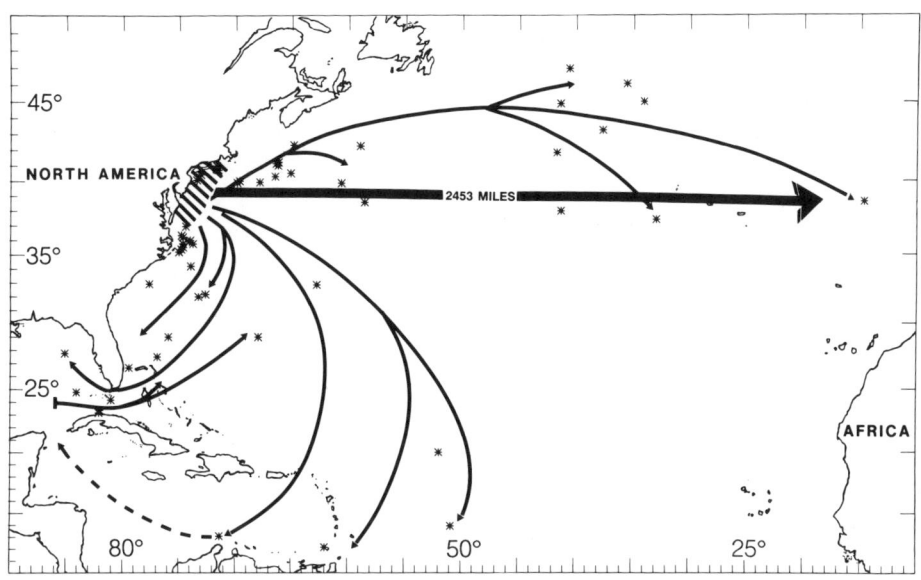

Mako shark returns from the North Atlantic Ocean (greater than 300 miles).

tance recorded for a tagged blue shark is 3,740 miles. Yet multiple recaptures suggest blue sharks may make round-trip movements between North America and Europe that exceed 10,000 miles. Sandbar sharks travelling on the continental shelf between Southern New England and Yucatan, Mexico, could easily cover 3,500 miles. On the other hand, a single long-distance recapture must be interpreted with caution since it may only reflect the stray movement of an individual shark outside the normal range of that species. For example, the oceanic whitetip shark is a highly pelagic species that is so rare in Hudson Canyon off New York that the fisherman who caught one provided a photograph of the shark being tagged to confirm the identification.

When interpreting tag-recapture data, consideration is also given to the possibility that the returns are more indicative of areas of intensive fishing, and the absence of recaptures in another area does not automatically rule out the possibility of sharks occurring there. The blue shark was considered rare in the Caribbean because it was known to be a temperate species that preferred cooler waters. However, expanding longline fisheries for tunas and swordfish in warmer regions of the Atlantic showed blue sharks to be common in the deeper offshore zones and around islands where upwelling brings cooler, deeper waters closer to the surface. Another consideration is that tagged sharks are sometimes recaptured in the same area where they were released several years earlier. Where a particular shark travelled during those years can be deduced only from other information. In addition, sharks generally segregate by size and sex, and the different segments of the population can have different migration patterns.

For these and other reasons, the NMFS long term tagging program can be likened to thousands of people working on an extremely complicated puzzle. The work is fascinating, challenging, and rewarding but at times frustrating because it requires a great deal of patience,

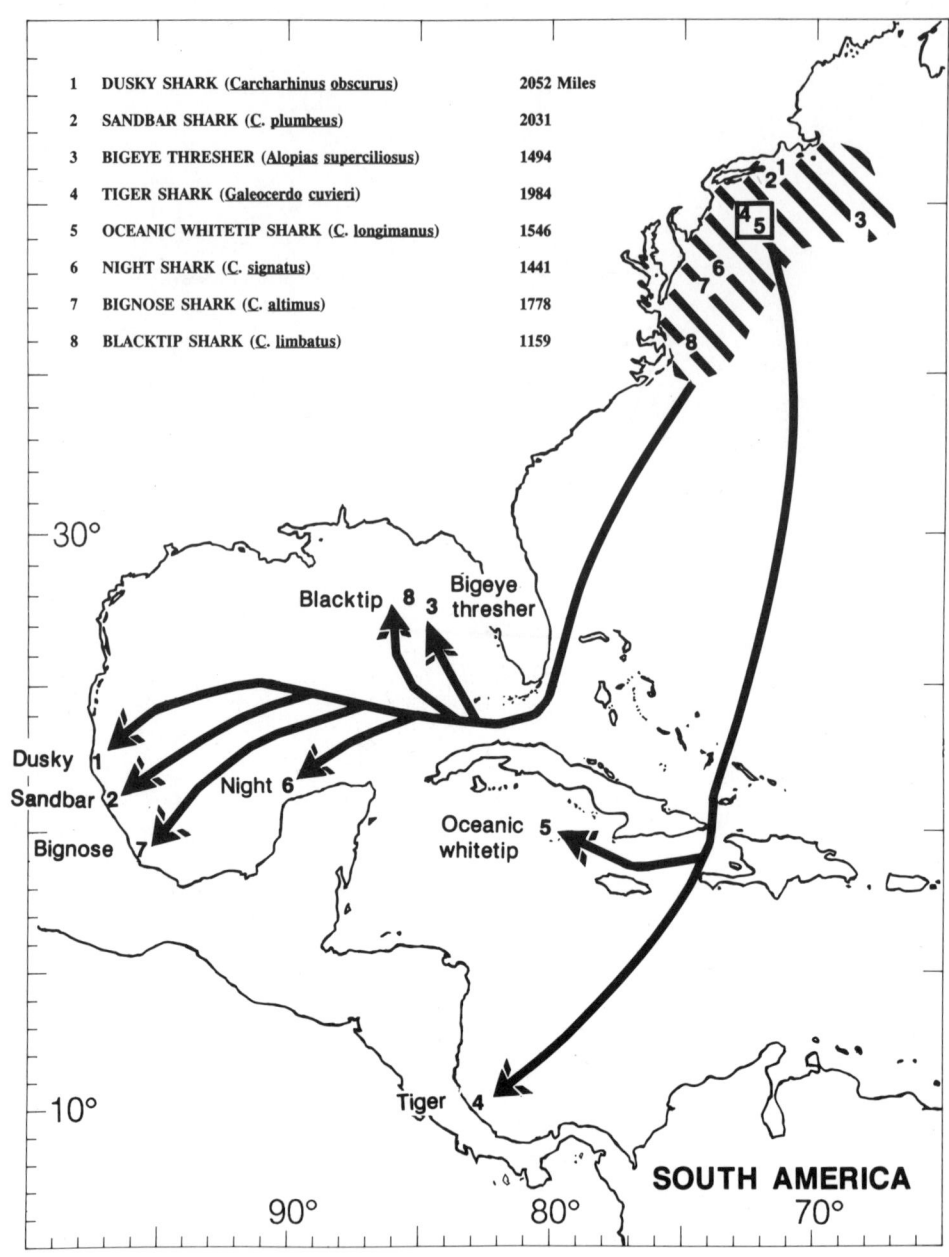

Maximum distances traveled by coastal pelagic sharks.

and the picture remains far from complete. The discovery of a new piece of scientific information from tagging, particularly if it involves a record of some kind, deserves special attention because it represents a focal point in the advancement of knowledge that is a credit to everyone past and present who has participated in the research.

In addition to contributing to the basic biological knowledge of sharks, this information demonstrating movements across international boundaries is important for shark management initiatives.

"Shark Management" in different parts of the world ranges from efforts to reduce shark populations where they are considered dangerous or represent costly nuisances to other fisheries, to maintaining populations at sustainable harvest levels for food and other uses. In Australia, conservation measures were enacted to protect shark populations in danger of serious depletion. During the past two decades sharks have become more important in U.S. recreational fisheries. Over the past 10 years, the recreational catch of Atlantic sharks has averaged about 4,000 metric tons. In recent years, sharks have also become important in U.S. commercial fisheries. Between 1987 and 1988, U.S. commercial landings of Atlantic sharks increased nearly threefold, from about 2,000 to 6,000 metric tons (Leach et al., 1989). These expanding sport and commercial fisheries have prompted sufficient concern for overfishing the stocks that a Fisheries Management Plan for Atlantic Sharks has been prepared by the Secretary of Commerce and is scheduled to go into effect in 1991. The fact that fishermen from many countries have returned NMFS tags from sharks released in U.S. waters can be used to argue for international management of highly pelagic species. Other Atlantic shark species might best be managed through cooperative action between Northern and Central American countries. Finally, the responsibility for some local shark populations may rest with a few, or even single states.

Whatever management directions are taken in the future, the success of those actions will depend on a better understanding of the biology of each shark species, including additional knowledge of their reproductive biology, food requirements, life spans, rates of growth, and migratory patterns. Fortunately, this knowledge continues to advance, and the pieces of the puzzle keep falling into place, bringing with them a clearer perspective of man's responsibility for sharks as living marine resources.

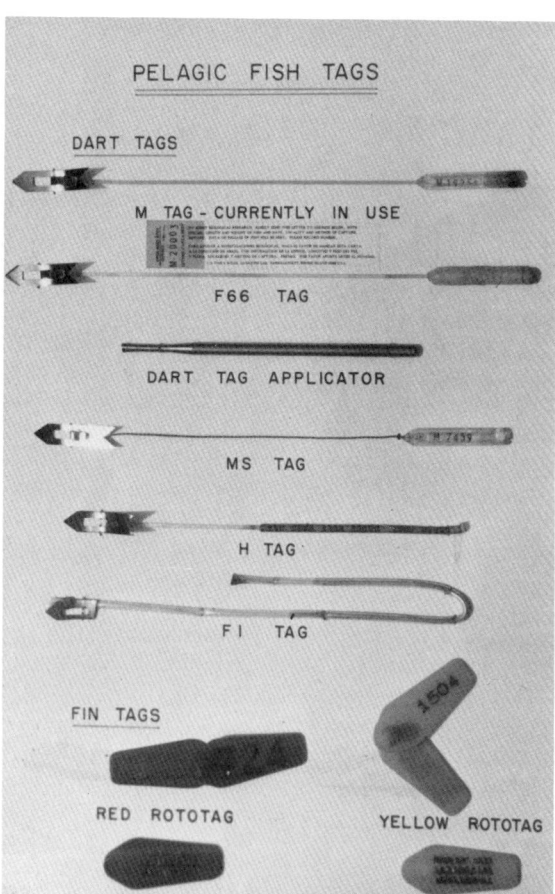

Dart and fin tags used on sharks by NMFS.

ADDITIONAL READING:

Casey, J.G. 1985. Transatlantic Migrations of the blue shark; a case history of cooperative shark tagging. pp. 253-268. *In* R.H. Stroud (Ed.) World Angling Resources and Challenges. Proceedings of the First World Angling Conference, Cap d'Agde, France, September 12 to 18, 1984. Int. Game Fish Assoc., Ft. Lauderdale, FL.

Leach, P., D. Hays, P. Hooker, P. Kurkul, J. Casey, J. Castro. 1989. Draft Secretarial Shark Fishery Management Plan for the Atlantic Ocean. NMFS NOAA Review Document, 116 pp.

THE BEHAVIOR OF SHARKS:
What Have We Learned?
by ARTHUR A. MYRBERG, JR. and DONALD R. NELSON

Due apparently to a general feeling that sharks were of little importance, progress in understanding their behavior was slow to almost non-existent until the late 1950's. Fortunately, a respected scientist and former shark fisherman who had also served as a manager of a shark-processing facility was around at that time; his name was Stewart Springer. In 1967, he published an admirable summary of the information known about the behavior and the social organization of sharks. That report provided not only a number of major scientific insights into the behavioral systems of sharks, but also stressed the importance of sharks to marine ecosystems and their high vulnerability to human exploitation.

Interest in shark behavior began growing in the late 1950's and continued through the '60's and '70's, due in large measure to the efforts of the Shark Research Panel of the American Institute of Biological Sciences and the financial support provided by the U.S. Office of Naval Research. During that 20 + year period a wealth of information was gained on numerous aspects of shark biology, but emphasis was particularly directed at the sensory worlds of sharks. Since understanding the behavior of any animal demands an understanding of the capabilities and the limitations of its sensory systems, the emphasis was well placed.

Since 1964 Myrberg has been on the faculty of the University of Miami's Rosenstiel School of Marine and Atmospheric Science. His interests include shark behavioral activities and the sensory biology of fishes. Nelson, a professor of biology at California State University, Long Beach, researches the behavior, ecology, and sensory biology of sharks and rays and specializes in field/underwater studies.

Responsiveness To Environmental Stimuli

It seems the clichéd name "swimming nose" was accurate, as sharks of several groups were found to be extremely responsive to several animal products, particularly proteins — their structural units (amino acids) as well as their breakdown products (amines). This was reflected well in the prey of those sharks. Evidence was also obtained that sharks have visual sensitivities equivalent to animals known to rely greatly on vision for their activities. Proof of color vision was obtained from one species, the lemon shark. Interestingly, the eyes of some species, including the lemon shark, are somewhat far-sighted. Why this is so remains a mystery.

Sharks were also found to have excellent hearing, albeit limited to frequencies below about 600 Hz (the fundamental of E below high C on the piano). However, their hearing range extends below 10 Hz, or well into the "infrasonic" range, so these predators can detect low-frequency disturbances beyond the range of human experience. Sharks have three sensory systems, inner ears, canal organs (lateral line), and "pit" organs, devoted to providing information on the direction of sound sources and hydrodynamic disturbances. Sound-playback experiments determined that the most attractive sounds were those resembling the hydrodynamic disturbances produced by struggling prey (hooked or speared fish, or fish seized by natural predators) or by erratically swimming fish (as in a frenzy of large fish feeding on small fish).

Sharks were also found to be like many other animals when it comes to high amplitude sounds in that they can be temporarily repelled or startled by sudden

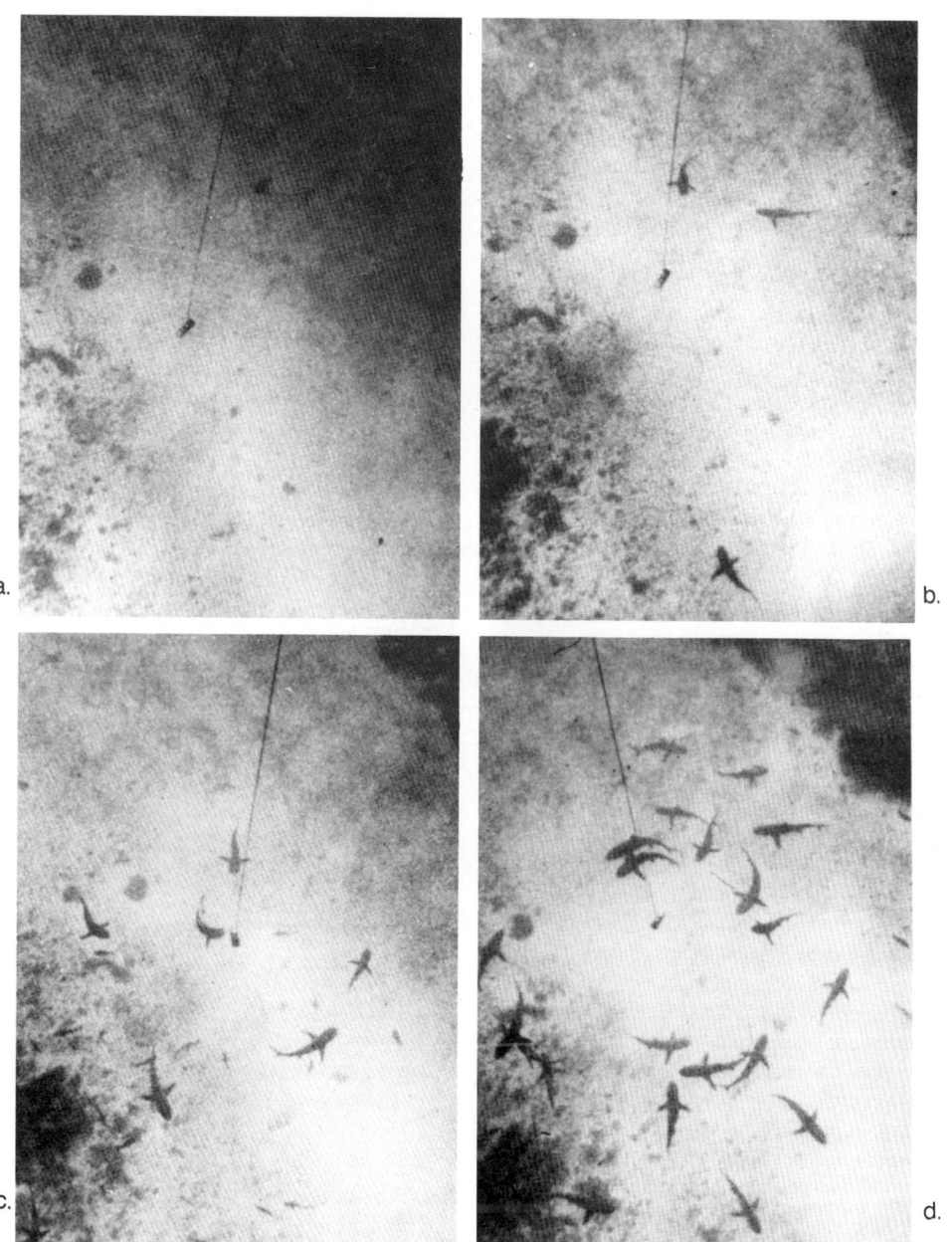

Attraction of gray reef sharks to underwater speaker emitting low-frequency, pulsed sound. (a.) at sound onset (b.) 10 seconds after onset (c.) 30 seconds after onset (shark about to bite speaker) (d.) two minutes after onset.

loud sounds, particularly those with levels 10 or more times above ambient. Such withdrawal responses were not consistent though. Large sharks were less responsive than small ones and some species, like silky sharks, were repeatedly repelled by repetitive sound presentations, while others like the oceanic whitetip, moved away only once or twice and subsequent presentations had no effect. SCUBA bubble noise also appeared to cause the rapid departure of schooling scalloped hammerheads during several underwater studies. Response was presumably due to the noise, but visual stimuli were not controlled.

Sharks and their near relatives, the skates and rays, hold one clear world record in the animal kingdom. No other animal has equalled their sensitivity to weak bio-and geoelectric fields, with detection thresholds as low as 0.005 uV/cm. Their exquisite capabilities enable sharks to locate and capture buried prey through the weak electric fields surrounding them which betray their presence. These capabilities also, theoretically, allow sharks to determine compass direction relative to the earth's magnetic field. Perhaps a shark can detect either the weak electric current induced within its body as it swims or the geoelectric fields produced in the surrounding ocean water as that parcel of water moves through the earth's magnetic field. Such a compass mechanism could help explain the numerous cases of long distance seasonal movements of sharks. Tagging studies show that species, such as the blue, mako, bigeye thresher, night, and tiger, cross enormous expanses of open ocean, while dusky, bignose, sandbar, bull, and blacktip sharks make coastal migrations of hundreds or even thousands of miles.

Less extensive, but highly oriented movements across deep water occur daily in some sharks, such as the scalloped hammerhead. Acoustical tracking has demonstrated such sharks homing to seamounts in the Sea of Cortez after nights of foraging in pelagic waters many miles away. Although such moves might be explained by the shark's "riding" currents or by following temperature gradients or "landmark" features, such explanations appear inadequate for all cases. The existence of an electromagnetic compass must be proven, of course, but evidence is accumulating as in recent studies of stingrays showing altered movement direction in response to artificially shifted electric fields.

Other orientational mechanisms are also likely, given the appropriate circumstances. For example, the daily movements of home-ranging lemon sharks in the shallow waters off Bimini, Bahamas, appear at least partly controlled by the position of the sun. Other cases of known recurrent daily and seasonal movements probably involve visual recognition of "underwater" landmarks, the recognition of familiar odors, or possibly homing to characteristic sounds. Geomagnetic anomalies have also been suggested as detectable shark landmarks. It is, thus, becoming apparent that sharks and their near relatives have a number of sophisticated orientational mechanisms that they can use to navigate over distances, short or long.

Learning

Testing the sensory capacities of captive sharks has also provided information on learning abilities. Sharks from several divergent families were readily trainable in both classical and operant conditioning procedures. Habituation, a simple form of learning, has also been noted during field tests of sensory function, such as in studies of attraction to low-frequency sounds. Knowledge of learning capabilities helps in understanding why behavioral differences exist among members of the same species. For example, juveniles are almost invariably more aggressive than adults. Their actions are also often more erratic and unpredictable than those of adults. Reasons for this are unknown, but the young of many animals modify their behavior through experience as they mature. This probably also holds true for sharks.

Activity Rhythms

The universality of rhythms in biological systems certainly extends to the behavior of sharks. Telemetry tracking experiments in the field have found daily rhythms of activity and directional movement among diverse groups including

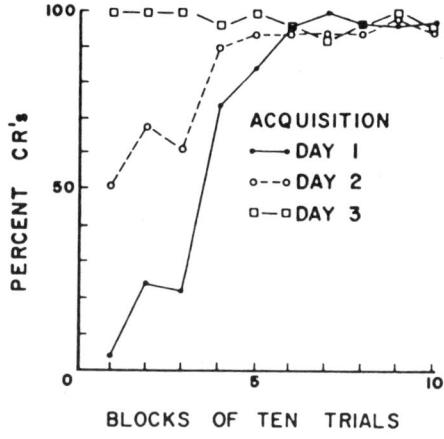

Course of acquisition of a classically conditioned movement of the eyelid by the lemon shark. Training consisted of pairing a flash of light with low voltage electric shock 100 times a day (10 blocks of 10 trials). The sharks reached nearly 100 % conditioned responses by 60th trial of the first day.

blue sharks, gray reef sharks, lemon sharks, scalloped hammerheads, and horn sharks. Well-documented studies showed blue sharks moving inshore during the early evening, then moving back offshore before dawn. Gray reef sharks, tracked offshore of Indo-Pacific coral atolls, often exhibited distinct differences between day and night ranges and also depths, moving between them at relatively predictable times.

All of these studies indicated a basically nocturnal pattern, with more activity, presumably foraging, occurring between dusk and dawn. Some evidence points to the actual peak of activity during the crepuscular (twilight) periods. Controlled laboratory experiments on California horn and swell sharks showed, under constant conditions of illumination, clear circadian rhythms of locomotor activity, that is, periodicities controlled by an internal endrogenous biological clock. Under artificial day-night regimes (12 hr light, 12 hr dark), these sharks, as well as lemon sharks from Florida, showed higher rates of movement during the night phase. Although such activity rhythms were scientifically documented only recently, experienced shark fishermen were not surprised; they had been using such knowledge for many years.

Social Activity and Aggression

Sharks have often been considered solitary rather than social creatures. Although this may be true for the adults of some large species, such as the white and tiger, grouping is actually quite common and often appears related to seasonal or diel cycles. In some instances, spectacular schools of large individuals can be observed, like those of the scalloped hammerheads found seasonally at offshore seamounts in the Sea of Cortez.

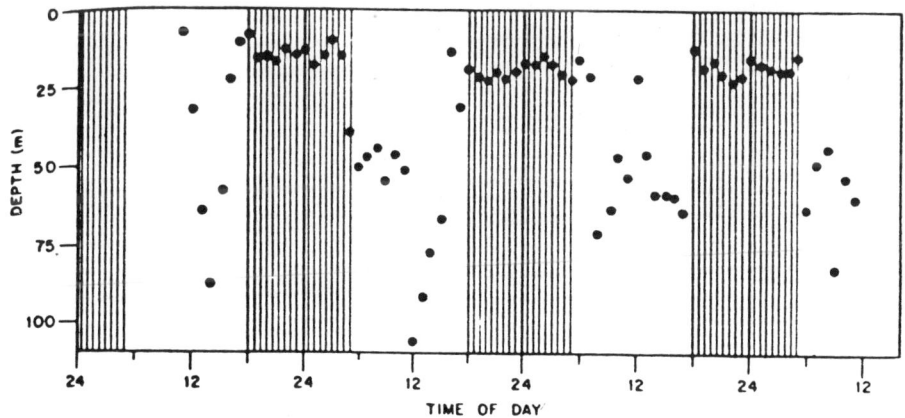

Rhythmic diurnal movements of one free-ranging, gray reef shark tracked continuously for 72 hours by acoustical telemetry in Rangroa, French Polynesia.

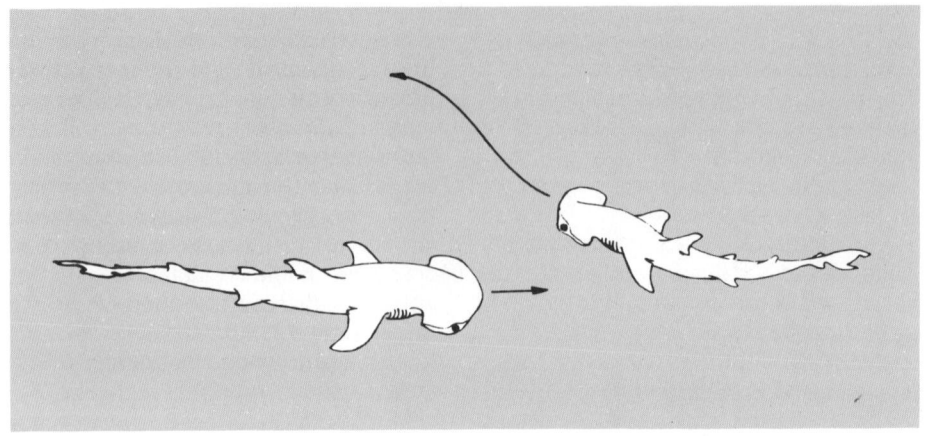

The action pattern give way in the bonnethead shark. Analysis of this pattern formed basis of the social hierarchy noted in a captive group.

It is axiomatic that when animals congregate in groups, social interactions will follow. We now know from well-documented studies of captive bonnethead and smooth dogfish sharks that dominance/subordinance hierarchies exist in small groups if held in large enclosures under semi-natural conditions. In the bonnethead study, there was a clear size-dependent rank order with an additional complication — an apparent shyness by females towards males of any size. The reason for this is unknown, but may be based on the courtship harassment and bite damage that male sharks normally inflict upon females during the mating period.

In his classic summary of 1967, Stewart Springer noted that interspecific (involving members of different species) social hierarchies exist in nature. He mentioned the dominance of oceanic whitetips over silky sharks, regardless of size, as well as the deference shown to hammerheads by most species. Similar interspecific relationships apparently exist among species of the coral reefs of the central Pacific, such as the gray reef shark's dominance over reef whitetip sharks. Interestingly, an individual's rank in a dominance order is generally established and maintained by aggressive actions between the individuals concerned. However, sharks rarely show overt aggression, which makes it difficult for the scientist to determine such relationships.

Perhaps this is due to inhibitions often found in species with formidable weapons (like teeth in the case of sharks) that could easily inflict fatal wounds on combatants — an idea first proposed by Konrad Lorenz. Thus, rank had to be established in other ways — in the case of the bonnethead study by "give ways," events where one individual moves out of the way of another. Aggression between conspecifics is rarely seen in the field. In the waters off Bimini, Bahamas, observers in low-flying, ultralight aircraft never witnessed overt aggression between the lemon sharks being studied. Large individuals would often encounter and approach others while moving about their home areas. The sharks then either slowly circled each other or followed in formations of two or more for a time before parting company. The significance of these behaviors is unknown.

Clear aggression is not unknown, however, among sharks. In gray reef sharks of the Indo-Pacific, apparently non-food-motivated attacks, prefaced by a pattern called exaggerated-swimming display, have been observed. This relatively stereotyped action involves the lifting of the snout, arching of the back, and lowering of the pectoral fins, while swimming in a tense, laterally exaggerated fashion.

This display is probably motivated by threat, such as the nearby presence of a larger animal (hammerhead shark), blocking avenues of escape (by divers), or thwarting feeding opportunities (by a large moray eel). Although in a number of instances, the display ended with an explosive attack, its cause remains unclear. In one study, a miniature submarine was used as a model to perform experimental approaches to gray reef sharks. Several such instances resulted in displays and attacks. In this case, the sharks appeared to regard the sub as a predator (antipredatory motivation) rather than as a competitor (defense of rank or territory), and definitely not as food (predatory motivation).

Members of some other species have shown less exaggerated forms of the above-mentioned display when suddenly confronted with large, strange objects or the presence of a nearby shark (both suggestive of antipredatory motivation). These species include the Galapagos, silky, lemon, and even the small bonnethead shark. In no such case did an attack follow the display. Nevertheless, it is noteworthy that this type of display occurs in various species, and that the situations are quite similar.

Courtship biting is another type of "aggression" that occurs between members of the same species. Adult females of a number of species show scars on their bodies from males biting them during mating activities. Some sharks have apparently evolved adaptations in response to this rather brutal mating behavior. The skin of female blue sharks is much thicker than that of males.

Males are not alone in their tendency to act aggressively towards conspecifics, however. Females in large aggregations

Exaggerated-swimming display of gray reef shark. Left column shows lateral, frontal, and dorsal view of shark in display. Right column shows same views of shark in non-display mode.

of scalloped hammerheads in the Sea of Cortez also inflict "hits," with resulting scars, on other females. Here the motivation may be female-female competition for mating access to the relatively scarce mature males. Actual mating (copulation) has not been seen in such instances.

When considering aggression, the phenomenon of territorial defense should be mentioned. Although territoriality in sharks is frequently implied in popular articles and TV documentaries, it must be stated that no conclusive evidence yet exists that any shark is territorial. By territory, behavioral scientists mean an area defended for purposes of exclusive use. This is in contrast to the concept of home range, a region over which an animal roams (regardless of whether it is defended or not). Many sharks are home ranging, but none have met the criteria for territoriality. Springer recognized this in 1967 and, despite numerous field studies since then, the situation has not changed. For any animal, defending a territory against intruders has a cost which must be exceeded by the benefits of exclusive use of the resources in that area. For sharks, with relatively large foraging-space requirements, the costs of defending such an area apparently do not justify the benefits.

The Feeding Frenzy

The feeding frenzy is another much publicized case of aggressive behavior. Under certain circumstances, individuals within groups develop a competitive feeding pattern, dashing about at high speed, biting any object in the vicinity, including at times, other individuals. At the height of a frenzy, any animal, shark or other, can be devoured. Conditions that trigger a frenzy usually include the presence of an unusual feeding opportunity (a large prey animal or otherwise large quantity of food) in conjunction with the phenomenon of social facilitation, which is the enhancement of behavior of one individual induced by the presence and behavior of other individuals. For example, let us consider the case of a dead or wounded whale emitting odorous stimuli attractive to sharks. When the first shark arrives, feeding may be delayed as this lone individual "sizes up" the prey. However, as competitors arrive, their individual activities act as a mutual catalyst for increasing the activities of all present. Hesitancy to approach the prey object diminishes with the arrival of additional sharks. When one shark eventually moves in for the first bite, this action serves as the trigger for the other sharks to abandon their hesitancy and rush in to feed.

Feeding frenzies are certainly not unique to sharks. They occur to varying degrees in many predatory species. Take for example, schooling tunas feeding on baitfish while seabirds feed on the same baitfish from above, or hyenas feeding on a recent kill. When it occurs in sharks, however, it can be especially impressive, perhaps because of their size and formidable dentition capable of removing large pieces of prey. Sometimes the frenzy develops an intensity where the participants seem "out of control," biting at anything in sight. As violent as the frenzy can sometimes be, it appears to be aggression in the broad sense only — a type of "scramble" competition where the objects of the attacks are the food items, not the competitive individuals. Other sharks may be the objects of attack in "contest" competition over food when one individual attacks or fights another not to eat, but to establish dominance and an unimpeded access to the food. One shark might bite another during a frenzy for this reason, but it seems more likely to be simply the misplaced feeding responses of overstimulated sharks.

In his 1967 report, Stewart Springer commented on the factor of motivation in sharks. He failed to find any indication of a hunger "drive" (our quotes) operating in sharks that was similar in nature to that experienced by humans. Several more recent studies on juvenile lemon sharks have shed light on this topic. They demonstrated not only specific rhythms of feeding activity but also that hunger, as defined objectively through periods of food deprivation, does indeed exist in sharks and has become a most useful tool for further studies of feeding behavior.

Communication

One aspect of social behavior that has long intrigued ethologists is how members of a given species communicate with one another, and what information is being transmitted. Although much is known about such things in many vertebrate animals, almost nothing is known about the subject in sharks. Yet, it's clear that communication must be very important to sharks, especially during the mating season when individuals must locate members of the opposite sex and presumably assess their reproductive status before copulation is possible.

Limited observations suggest that males of certain reef sharks use odor trails to locate females. Whether specific communicative chemicals, such as pheromones, are involved has not been established, but seems a likely possibility. In terms of visual signals, recent evidence suggests that the species-specific fin markings of many requiem sharks are used for species recognition. Interestingly, in the case of the oceanic whitetip shark, its large white fin tips may also serve as lures to attract its fast-moving prey into capture range. The various display postures of sharks, such as the exaggerated-swimming pattern of gray reef sharks and the corkscrew-swim of scalloped hammerheads, are likely also visual signals, but their intraspecific functions have yet to be determined. The lack of knowledge about social communication clearly points to a field wide open for study.

The White Shark — An Enigma

Although science continues to chip away the ignorance surrounding many aspects of shark behavior, little has been revealed about the behavior of the most fearsome of all, the white shark. There is no question that this large shark is responsible for the great majority (if not all) of the attacks on humans in areas such as central and northern California and southern Australia. The normal prey of adult white sharks includes marine mammals such as harbor seals, sea lions, and even elephant seals — all animals that equal or exceed the size of human swimmers. It is, thus, not hard to envision a white shark striking a dark suited diver or surfer on a short board as part of its normal predatory behavior. However, the white shark is more of a man-biter than a man-eater, with most strikes resulting in the shark releasing and not re-attacking its human victim. It has never been confirmed that the shark actually consumed a person. Herein lies the

White shark. Cousteau Society Photo.

White shark. Cousteau Society Photo.

controversy. Why does the white shark release, rather than consume its human victims?

One theory maintains that the attack is a strike due to mistaken identity. The shark attacks because the person resembles a seal; then the shark releases the person when it senses that it is not. Another theory maintains that the normal predatory behavior is a "bite-and-spit" pattern, in which the shark, after inflicting an initial massive wound, backs off to let the victim expire before returning to consume it. A third theory, that the shark bites as a territorial warning to a competitor, has little basis in fact. A territorial individual normally gives a threat display before attacking. A white shark attacks without warning, from below and behind, as would be expected for a predator stalking a prey.

Most of our knowledge of white shark feeding behavior in the wild comes from observations of opportunistic feeding, such as sharks scavenging on dead whales, or from highly artificial baited situations where divers in cages observe and film the sharks. What is known about the white shark's normal predatory behavior? Recently, scientists working at the Farallon Islands (off San Francisco) have observed natural predation on seals and sea lions. From high vantage points on the rocky islands, a catalog of videotaped predatory incidents is being accumulated. Analysis of these attacks should help resolve the controversy over whether the "bite-and-spit" pattern is normal for white sharks.

Behavioral Studies — A Bright Future

Considering that sharks are generally wide-roaming, secretive in their ways, and fragile when held under captive conditions, we have learned quite a bit about their behavior and related subjects. Yet, it's also obvious that we should know much more. While government financial support for behavioral studies has diminished in recent years, public awareness and interest in these intriguing animals has remained high, and a conservation ethic is beginning to emerge. Young workers can be assured that the study of sharks and their behavior will be a fertile area for scientific investigation well into the future.

ADDITIONAL READING:

Gruber, S.H. & A.A. Myrberg, Jr. 1977. Approaches to the study of the behavior of sharks. American Zoologist 17:471-486.

Myrberg, Jr., A.A. 1987. Understanding shark behavior. p. 41-83. In: Sharks: an Inquiry into Biology, Behavior, Fisheries, and Use. S. Cook (ed.). Oregon State University Extension Service.

Nelson, D.R. 1977. On the field study of shark behavior. American Zoologist. 17:501-507.

Nelson, D.R. 1981. Aggression in sharks: is the gray reef shark different? Oceanus 24 (4):45-55.

Springer, V.G. & J.P. Gold 1989. SHARKS IN QUESTION. Smithsonian Institution Press, Washington, D.C.

Stevens, J.D. (ed.) 1987. SHARKS. Facts on File Publishers. New York, N.Y.

Shark Attack and the International Shark Attack File

by GEORGE H. BURGESS

Say the word "shark" and the first image most people conjure up is a *Jaws*-inspired white shark devouring unsuspecting bathers while well-meaning authorities and scientists helplessly stand by. Shark attack is probably man's most feared natural danger, surpassing even hurricanes, tornadoes, and earthquakes. Among the earth's large animals implicated in the attack and consumption of humans, only sharks have not been "controlled" by man. Even the fiercest terrestrial predators, the large cats and bears, are susceptible to a rifle, and "problem" animals have simply been eliminated, leaving many species endangered. Some crocodilians, especially the Nile and saltwater crocodiles, are certainly as dangerous as sharks, but these reptiles have never captured as much "press" in part because their populations are largely limited to Third World countries and they, too, are vulnerable to human hunting pressure. The sea's only other creatures capable of consuming a human, killer and sperm whales, are normally not considered threats. Sharks, on the other hand, have throughout recorded history been documented as attackers (and sometime consumers) of humans around the world, and they have remained relatively immune from human intervention.

Shark attack was not of particular public interest until the twentieth century. Several factors contributed to the

Director of the International Shark Attack File and senior biologist in ichthyology at the Florida Museum of Natural History, University of Florida, Gainesville, Burgess is a past president of the American Elasmobranch Society. His research interests include shark conservation, the systematics of deep-sea dogfish sharks, and life history and ecology of nearshore sharks, as well as shark attacks.

upswing in public awareness during the last 50-60 years. First and foremost is the evolution of the press from a parochial to a cosmopolitan news-gathering system that now covers a larger portion of the world more rapidly and comprehensively. Increased competition and a shift in some journalistic values have contributed to more active searches for "shock" stories that titillate the public and promote sales. An examination of current weekly tabloids confirms that "shark eats man" is a best-selling story line. The plethora of World War II air and sea disasters regrettably spawned the largest ever number of shark attacks and spurred research to find an effective shark repellent. The current worldwide trend towards more intense recreational use of marine waters has also increased the chances of shark-human interactions, resulting in an increase in the total number of attacks. Add the fictionalized shark accounts in the popular press and movies, and it's easy to see why shark attack is a hot topic.

The International Shark Attack File

The United States Navy has traditionally had more than a passing interest in shark attack since its personnel, particularly in wartime, face a greater risk of attack. Memories of the many documented attacks on World War II servicemen and the realization that an effective repellent was still unavailable prompted the Office of Naval Research to fund a shark-related research program in 1958. A conference was held early that year in New Orleans to plan a research strategy for development of an effective repellent. Participants agreed that much basic research was required before a repellent could be discovered, and a working group of shark researchers was formalized. The Shark Research Panel,

White shark. Cousteau Society Photo.

consisting of Perry W. Gilbert (chairman), Sidney R. Galler, John R. Olive, Leonard P. Schultz, Stewart Springer, and later Albert L. Tester and H. David Baldridge, remained active until 1970. The panel initiated the Shark Attack File, the first such attempt to comprehensively document attacks on a global, historical basis.

The Shark Attack File was housed at the Smithsonian Institution under the supervision of Schultz and a similar, smaller file was maintained by Gilbert at Cornell University. Attempts were made to collect data on all historical shark attacks, and a network of reporters was established to document new attacks as they occurred. Gilbert was able to secure institutional funding for news clipping services. A two-page attack reporting form was developed by the panel and made available to file cooperators. The file soon grew to over 1000 attacks.

The first attempt to synthesize the file's data was made by Schultz in 1963. His analysis, *Attacks by sharks as related to activities of man*, and accompanying appendix, *A list of shark attacks for the world* (coauthored by Marilyn H. Malin), appeared in SHARKS AND SURVIVAL, the first of two of Gilbert-edited volumes emanating from the Navy's support of shark research. Schultz realized, however, that such manual analyses were far too time consuming and more sophisticated methods were required. In 1967 the panel agreed that a computerized statistical analysis was needed and, with Naval funding, Baldridge produced his classic 1974 analysis entitled *Shark attack: a program of data reduction and analysis*.

Naval support ceased in 1968. Efforts made by Baldridge and Gilbert to secure funding from traditional sources were unsuccessful, and the file was later transferred from Mote Marine Laboratory, where it had been sent for Baldridge's analyses, to the University of Rhode Island. The file continued to grow under the care of John McAniff of the National Undersea Safety Program, but regrettably funding was unobtainable here too, despite McAniff's best efforts. In 1988 the file was transferred to the Florida Museum of Natural History, under the auspices of the American Elasmobranch Society, where it is now curated by the author.

The file is receiving enthusiastic support from members of the Society, an international organization of scientists actively engaged in the studies of sharks, skates, rays and chimaeras. Efforts are now underway to fill in many missing attack records for the 1968-1988 period. With the cooperation of the organization's many worldwide members, the file is growing, with large data bases from Australia, California, Hawaii, and South Africa added or soon to be integrated into the system. Baldridge's reduced data, formerly stored on long-lost computer punch cards, have been graciously made available to me and transferred from a computer print-out into a state-of-the-art data base system by Jeffrey C. Carrier.

We are currently attempting to document attacks from the largely incomplete 1968-1988 period as well as investigate new ones. We welcome unsolicited documentation of any attack from all time periods. Newly acquired data will be added as they appear, and periodic analyses of the data base will be performed to determine trends in local and world-wide attacks. The data base is also available to qualified biologists and physicians who wish to address specific questions regarding shark attack. Since the file contains much information that is considered privileged, such as medical reports, autopsies, and personal interviews, access is carefully guarded by a panel of AES shark researchers who must approve each request on a case-by-case basis. Inquiries from the media and general public are answered by the author, but actual access to the files is otherwise limited to scientists.

How, When, and Where

Worldwide there are probably 50-75 shark attacks annually resulting in about 5-10 deaths. I say probably because not all shark attacks are reported. Our information from Third World countries is especially poor, and in other areas attacks are sometimes kept quiet for fear of bad publicity. Historically the death rate was much higher, but the advent of readily available emergency services and improved medical treatment has greatly reduced the chances of mortality. Actual numbers of shark attacks may be going up because of increasing numbers of bathers, but there is no indication of any change in the per capita attack rate.

Most attacks occur in nearshore waters, typically inshore of a sandbar or between sandbars where sharks can be trapped at low tide. Areas with steep dropoffs are also likely attack sites. Sharks congregate in these areas because their natural food items also congregate there.

There are three major kinds of unprovoked shark attacks. By far the most common are "hit and run" attacks. These typically occur in the surf zone with swimmers and surfers the normal targets. The victim seldom sees its attacker, and the shark does not return after inflicting a single bite or slash wound. In most instances, these attacks are probably cases of mistaken identity that occur in poor water visibility and a harsh physical environment (breaking surf and strong wash/current conditions). A feeding shark in this habitat must make quick decisions and rapid movements to capture its traditional food items. When these difficult physical conditions are considered in conjunction with provocative human activities associated with aquatic recreation (splashing, shiny jewelry, colored swimsuits, contrasting tanning, especially involving the soles of the feet), it is not surprising that sharks might occasionally misinterpret a human for its normal prey. I suspect that, upon biting, the shark quickly realized that the human is a foreign object, or that it is too large, and immediately releases the victim and does not return. Some of these attacks could also be related to social behaviors unrelated to feeding, such as dominance behaviors seen in many land animals. Injuries to "hit and run" victims are usually confined to relatively small lacerations, often on the leg below the knee, and are seldom life-threatening.

"Bump and bite" and "sneak" attacks, while less common, result in greater injuries and the most fatalities. These types of attack usually involve divers or swimmers in deeper waters. "Bump and bite" attacks are characterized by the shark circling and often bumping the victim prior to the actual attack. "Sneak" attacks occur without warning. In both cases, unlike "hit and run" attacks, repeat attacks are not uncommon and multiple or sustained bites are the norm. Injuries incurred during this type of attack are usually quite severe, frequently resulting in death. I believe these types of attack are the result of feeding or agonistic behaviors rather than cases of mistaken identity. Most shark attacks involving sea disasters, such as plane and ship accidents, probably involve "bump and bite" and "sneak" attacks.

Almost any large shark, roughly six feet or longer, is a potential threat to humans. Three species, however, have been repeatedly implicated as the primary attackers: the white shark, *Carcharodon carcharias*, tiger shark, *Galeocerdo cuvieri*, and bull shark *Carcharhinus leucas*. All are cosmopolitan in distribution, reach large sizes, and consume large prey items such as marine mammals, sea turtles, and fishes as normal elements of their diets. These species probably are responsible for a large portion of "bump and bite" and "sneak" attacks. Other species, including the great hammerhead, mako, oceanic whitetip, Galapagos, and perhaps certain reef sharks have been implicated in these styles of attacks. We know less about the offending parties in "hit and run" cases since the shark is seldom observed, but it is safe to assume that a large suite of species might be involved. Circumstantial evidence from Florida, which has 10-15 of this type of attack per year, suggests that spinner (and possibly blacktip) sharks are the major culprits.

Shark attack is a potential danger that must be acknowledged by anyone frequenting marine waters, but it should be kept in perspective. Bees, wasps, and snakes are responsible for far more fatalities each year. In the United States the annual risk of death from lightning is 30 times greater than that from shark attack. Most shark-human interaction is likely to occur while swimming or surfing in nearshore waters. From a statistical standpoint the chances of dying in this area are markedly higher from other causes, such as drowning and cardiac arrest, than from shark attack. Many more people are injured and killed on land while driving to and from the beach than by sharks in the water. Shark attack trauma is also less common than such beach-related injuries as spinal damage, dehydration, jellyfish and stingray stings, and sunburn. Indeed, many more sutures are expended on pop-top lacerations than shark bites.

Nevertheless, certain risks are part of any recreational activity or sport: jogging offers shin splints, camping brings ticks and mosquitoes, tennis may result in sprained ankles, and so on. Beach recreation has its inherent risks as well, and shark attack is simply one of them. Most people agree, however, that there is an extremely slim chance of even encountering a shark, much less being bitten by one.

Reducing the Risk

Risks should be minimized whenever possible in any activity. The chances of interacting with a shark can be reduced if one heeds the following advice:

- Always stay in groups since sharks are more likely to attack a solitary swimmer.
- Do not wander too far from shore where you will be isolated and far away from assistance.
- Avoid the water during darkness or twilight hours when sharks are most active and have a competitive sensory advantage.
- Do not enter the water if bleeding from an open wound or if menstruating — a shark's olfactory ability is acute.
- Do not wear shiny jewelry because it reflects light and resembles the sheen of fish scales.
- Avoid waters with known effluents or sewage and those being used by sport or commercial fishermen, especially if there are signs of bait fishes or feeding activity. Diving seabirds are good indicators of such action.
- Porpoise sightings do not indicate the absence of sharks — both often eat the same food items.
- Use extra caution when waters are murky and avoid uneven tanning and bright colored clothing — sharks see contrast particularly well.
- Refrain from excess splashing and do not allow pets in the water because of their erratic movements.
- Exercise caution when occupying areas between sandbars or near steep dropoffs as these are favorite hangouts for sharks.
- Do not enter the water if sharks are known to be present and evacuate the water if sharks are sighted. And, of course, do not harass a shark if you see one.

NOTE: The American Elasmobranch Society is very interested in updating the International Shark Attack File. If you know of an attack, particularly from the 1968-1988 period, please forward documentation or contact the author at the following address: International Shark Attack File, Florida Museum of Natural History, University of Florida, Gainesville, FL 32611. Phone (904) 392-1721, FAX (904) 392-8783.

Mature white shark caught off Montauk, Long Island. Photo by H.L. Pratt.

SHARK REPELLENTS:
How Effective, How Needed?

by DONALD R. NELSON

Researchers are often asked about shark repellent development. Does a "practical" shark repellent exist? When is protection from sharks really needed? What about the typical recreational diver interested in just observing or photographing marine life?

Although not all are repellents per se, various antishark devices have been invented, including: *armor*, such as the stainless-steel chainmail suit; *weapons*, like the explosive powerhead and gas-injection dart; *stimulus screens*, such as the Shark Screen (plastic bag with inflatable collar); and *barriers*, like the antishark cage. But in the strict sense, a *repellent*, the opposite of an attractant, is something which drives a shark away, i.e., causes it to move away from or avoid the source.

The original "Shark Chaser" packet developed hurriedly during World War II was intended as a chemical repellent, but it has since proven ineffective. Nonchemical repellent devices include the physical prod (shark billy), the electric prod (modified cattle prod), and the electric Shark Shield (pulsed electric-field generator).

Since the Shark Chaser failure, the chemical approach to shark repellents had been in disfavor for two main reasons, (1) the great dispersion/dilution effect acting over time on any cloud of chemical in the open sea, and (2) the danger to the human user from chemicals noxious enough to repel sharks effectively. In 1972, however, Dr. Eugenie Clark

Nelson, a professor of biology at California State University, Long Beach, researches the behavior, ecology, and sensory biology of sharks and rays and specializes in field/underwater studies. He and his students have participated in shark research expeditions to the Gulf of California, the Bahamas, French Polynesia, Micronesia, and Australia.

found that a milky secretion from a Red Sea flatfish, the Moses sole, was highly repellent to sharks. The discovery prompted a renewed interest in chemical repellents. This time the emphasis was on natural biologically active substances.

Chemical analyses of the Moses sole secretion showed the active component to be a complex protein (pardaxin) which is difficult to isolate or synthesize. Even the crude secretion was costly to collect, unstable over time, and thus impractical as a repellent for general use. Researchers noticed, however, that like several other natural repellent substances, the material possessed surfactant (detergent) properties which were damaging to cell membranes. Playing a hunch, Drs. Eliahu Zlotkin and Samuel Gruber tested the sole extract against several commercial surfactants to see if any would mimic the action of the natural repellent. The tests were conducted at the University of Miami, using small captive lemon sharks. One particular compound, sodium dodecyl sulfate (SDS), showed promise. It repelled as well or better than the sole secretion (dried/redissolved), was relatively harmless to humans, and was available at low cost. We then began field tests on blue sharks in California to determine the effectiveness of this surfactant during experimental man-shark encounters in the open sea.

How effective is the surfactant chemical for actual use by a diver facing a bait-attracted shark? To answer this, we must distinguish between two ways of presenting the repellent, (1) the classical *surrounding cloud* method, and (2) the *directed squirt* method. In the first, the person swirls the chemical around him to create a protective cloud in which he must remain. With time, the cloud disperses outward (especially in rough

*Diver with squirt apparatus used to test chemical repellents on blue sharks.
Photo by L. Tillim.*

water), and must be periodically renewed to maintain the needed concentration. This method was intended primarily for people remaining in one spot, such as air/sea disaster survivors awaiting rescue on the surface.

How potent does a repellent have to be for surrounding cloud use? Naval scientists David Baldridge and Scott Johnson calculated that the chemical would have to be effective at a concentration of about 0.1 ppm (parts per million) — otherwise it would not last long enough and/or the quantity required would be too much to carry. At California State University, Long Beach, Larry Smith conducted laboratory swim-through tests on horn and swell sharks using sodium lauryl sulfate (SLS), a less-pure commercial form of SDS. In a special roundabout test tank, the sharks were made to swim into sections of water containing the uniformly dispersed chemical, simulating a surrounding cloud. Thresholds for useful repellency were roughly 100 ppm, three orders of magnitude (1000x) greater than deemed necessary by Baldridge and Johnson. The surfactant is thus not nearly potent enough for use in the surrounding cloud method.

In the directed squirt method, a relatively concentrated dose of repellent is presented to the shark. It requires a clear underwater view, so that the person can deliver an accurate shot into the face or mouth of the shark, using some type of squirt applicator. This method would be useful primarily for face-mask equipped swimmers or divers, and possibly life-raft occupants. Using air-powered syringe guns, our diver trials show that SLS is effective in repelling bait-attracted blue sharks if delivered into the mouth cavity at a concentration of several percent. A 250 ml shot of 5 to 10% SLS into the mouth of a six-foot blue shark nearly always resulted in mouth gaping, head-shaking, and departure from sight at accelerated speed.

In comparison to other classes of repellents tested, the chemical squirt resulted in a more permanent departure of the repelled shark. A vigorous prod with a shark billy usually caused a blue shark to retreat, but tests showed that it

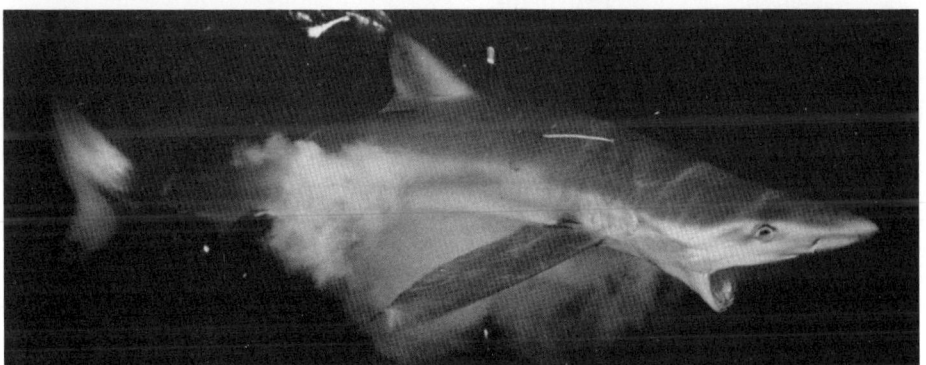

*Mouth gaping and rapid departure of a blue shark in response to a surfactant repellent.
Photo by L. Tillim.*

would often soon circle back. An electric-field pulser (Shark Shield) also turned away the shark which responded with a muscular flinch to each pulse. However, the shark readily returned to the bait after it left the immediate area where it could feel the pulses.

Who really needs to carry a shark repellent or other deterrent device? The survivor of an air/sea disaster, often injured, bleeding, far from land, and facing hours or days in the water before rescue, is obviously at risk (and not only from sharks). The now defunct Shark Chaser chemical packet was intended for this special situation. There is still no adequate repellent chemical for this type of surrounding-cloud application. The Shark Screen plastic bag (which folds into a small packet) or, better yet, a small life raft is the device of choice for such survival situations.

Does the ordinary recreational, scientific, or commercial diver need shark protection? This, of course, depends on the situation, but comes down to a personal decision of cost vs benefit. How much benefit (shark-risk reduction) justifies how much cost — not just the monetary cost, but the added complication, encumbrance, and even danger from the device itself? In most diving situations where an occasional shark sighting is to be expected, experienced divers (the author included) usually consider a cumbersome antishark device not worth the bother. At the other extreme, few divers would enter the water with baited white sharks without the protection of a shark cage, a major piece of anti-shark hardware. Spearfishing increases the shark-encounter risk due to the attractive sounds and smells produced by the wounded fish. The spearfisherman is usually not without protection, however, as even a discharged speargun can be used as a shark billy. In southern California, diver/photographers often deliberately enter the water with aggregations of baited blue and mako sharks. This is a moderately risky situation, and a number of divers have received bites (most relatively minor). When not in cages, these divers usually work in pairs, with the cameraman guarded by a safety diver armed with a shark billy or powerhead weapon. Several professional filmmakers use armored chain mail suits which are expensive but provide good protection against blue shark bites.

Probably the simplest repellent device of real value for the diver is the shark billy, a short pole (wooden or otherwise) used to push away or fend off a shark that comes too close. A billy is the recommended minimum protection in situations where sharks are likely to approach closely, such as baited blue sharks and gray reef sharks in remote areas. More protection is provided by a powerhead weapon, a pole tipped with a cartridge-detonating device. Unarmed, it can be used as a billy. When armed, it becomes a lethal firearm. The question is then whether such firepower justifies the risk of accidental discharge and injury to the user, or the unnecessary destruction of the shark. A shark billy might also be equipped with a non-lethal chemical or electrical repellent. For example, a chemically enhanced shark billy could be produced that would, if needed, allow the diver to squirt repellent at a persistent shark that refuses to be discouraged by physical action alone.

ADDITIONAL READING:

Baldridge, D. 1974. SHARK ATTACK. Droke House/Hallux, Inc., Anderson, S.C. (also Berkley Medallion Books, N.Y. 263 p.)

Clark, E. 1974. The Red Sea's sharkproof fish. National Geographic Magazine 145(5):718-727.

Gruber, S., Zlotkin, E., and D. Nelson. 1984. Shark repellents: Behavioral bioassays in laboratory and field. Pages 26-42 in Bolis, L., and J. Zadunaisky, Toxins, Drugs, and Pollutants in Marine Animals, Springer-Verlag, Berlin.

Nelson, D.R. 1983. Shark attack and repellency research: An overview. Pages 11-74 in B. Zahuranec, ed., Shark Repellents from the Sea: New Perspectives. AAAS Selected Symposium Series, Westview Press, Boulder, CO.

Perrine, D. 1989. Reef shark attack! Sea Frontiers 35(1):31-41

Uncovering the Ages of Sharks and Its Importance in Fisheries Management

by CHARLES S. PIKE III

Sharks are important to the ecology of our world's oceans. Most sharks occupy the top level in the food chain, exerting a strong control over the other fish species present in the environment. Their longevity and diversity make them some of nature's most amazing animals. Sharks have been in the world's oceans for over 350 million years. Today there are over 375 known species of living sharks, and over half of these species are of some importance to fisheries.

Historically, there have been few shark fisheries in the United States. Until recently, sharks were an underutilized resource taken only in small, localized fisheries such as the spiny dogfish (*Squalus acanthias*) fishery off California in the late 1930's and 1940's; the soupfin (*Galeorhinus zyopterus*) fishery, off Oregon and Washington from 1940 to 1949; and the porbeagle (*Lamna nasus*) fishery, on Newfoundland Banks during the 1960's. Commercial and recreational interest has led to an increased demand, and new fisheries were developed in the 1980's as a result of domestic demand for shark meat and a foreign demand for shark fins.

Slow growth rates, low rates of reproduction, and a close relationship between stock size and recruitment typically contribute to a rapid decline in shark numbers soon after exploitation begins. Thus, shark fisheries are susceptible to overfishing. Exploitation of a single shark species inevitably leads to rapid decline of stocks and sooner or later a dramatic collapse of the fishery. Evidence is quickly accumulating on the delicate nature of these animals. They are important to marine ecosystems, susceptible to overexploitation and rapid depletion, and valuable as food sources and biomedical research subjects. Further biological and life history information, knowledge on stock status, and responses to fishing are desperately required so the resources can be effectively managed. The core of any management plan is an assessment of the stock which depends on the accurate estimation of the age structure of each species.

Age and growth data are central to every comprehensive fish population study. Information which can be secured from aging fishes includes growth rate, age at maturity, number of spawning periods per life span, age at harvest, age class composition of catch, abundance of year classes, longevity, and mortality rate. These data can be used for fishery management in the following ways: 1) to provide general background needed for management decisions; 2) to help diagnose management needs; 3) to evaluate the effects of management practices; 4) to estimate optimum yields and the possible effects of catch regulations through the use of growth and mortality rates; 5) to predict catch from year class abun-

A marine biology doctoral candidate at the University of Miami's Rosenstiel School of Marine and Atmospheric Science, Pike is researching age and growth, calcium physiology, and population dynamics of sharks.

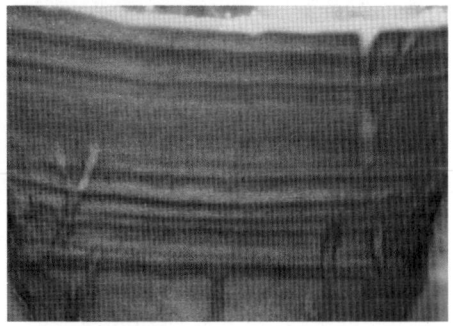

Photomicrograph of a stained centrum section from a juvenile lemon shark.
Photo by C. Pike.

dance; and 6) to determine production rates using additional estimates of population numbers. Age and growth information can provide insight into a species' ability to sustain a fishery, as well as contribute to understanding a species' role in its ecosystem.

Little is known about the age and growth of sharks because many species are difficult to sample, are of relatively large size, are highly mobile, are of minor commercial value, or are present geographically only at certain times of the year. Several methods of variable reliability exist for estimating the age of sharks. These include: 1) plotting the sizes of the sharks caught in the fishery and assigning age classes to the peaks in the distribution (length frequency); 2) observing the degree of calcification at the edge of the vertebral centra (centrum edge analysis); 3) recording peaks of calcium and phosphorus concentrations in the centra and correlating these with growth rings; and 4) counting the number of calcified rings which are deposited in the vertebral centra of the shark as it ages — this being the most promising method. Centra calcify in a cyclic manner producing ring patterns that alternate between high and reduced calcium content. Validation studies, using tetracycline hydrochloride injections as a time marker, have shown that these rings are deposited on a regular basis, so it is possible to estimate the age of a shark by counting the number of rings. To confidently interpret the meaning of ring counts, it must be demonstrated that ring formation provides a continuous record of growth and that the count represents known intervals of time.

In our research on lemon sharks (*Negaprion brevirostris*) at the University of Miami, the vertebrae are soaked and cleaned in diluted chlorine bleach and oven dried. Vertebral centra are cut in half and a 3 mm thick section is cut from this half-section. The sections are ground down to 150 um and then stained in alizarin red S, a stain specific for calcium. More stain is absorbed by the highly calcified rings, giving an alternating band pattern. The sections are viewed under a compound microscope and the number of rings counted. This method is similar to counting the rings in the trunk of a tree to determine its age.

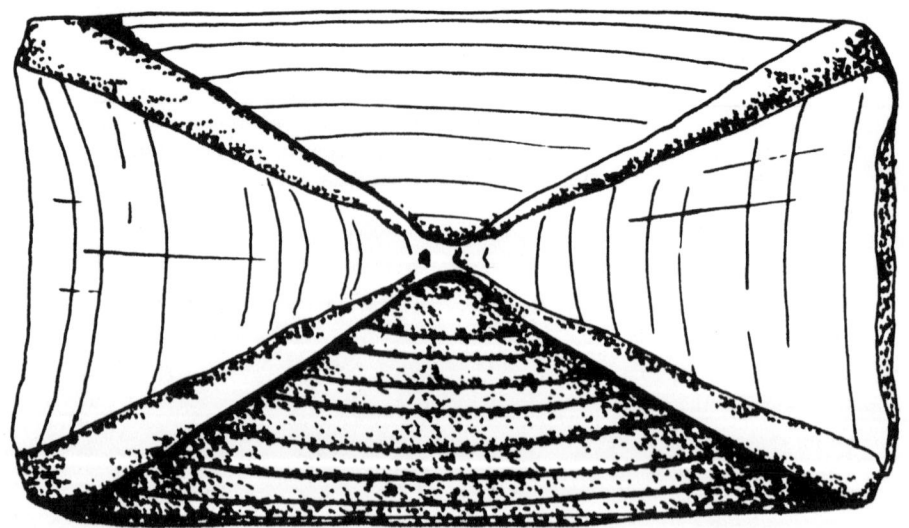

Tracing of projected image of stained vertebral centrum (lateral cross section) from a subadult lemon shark.

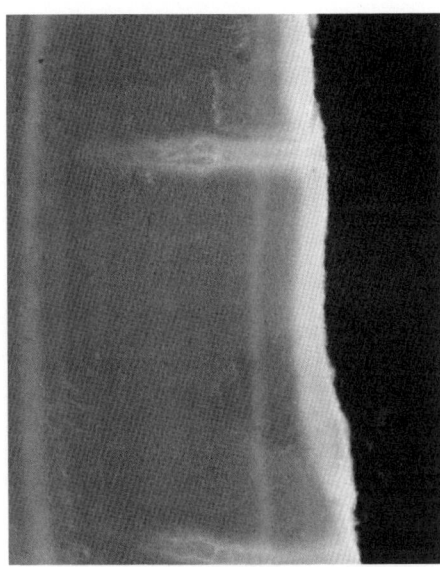

Photomicrograph of unstained centrum section (under ultraviolet light) from juvenile lemon shark showing two tetracycline markers. Photo by C. Pike.

Validation is a very important part of any aging study. As previously noted, the most reliable validation technique involves injecting the sharks with the antibiotic, tetracycline hydrochloride at the beginning of the study. The tetracycline is taken up and deposited at sites of active calcification, producing a reference mark reflecting the time of injection. When the centrum section is viewed under ultraviolet light, the number of rings which are deposited beyond the tetracycline marker can be compared to the known elapsed time to validate the time increment.

We have had great success in elucidating vertebral rings which occur not only on a yearly basis but also more frequently (every 31 days in the wild and every 62 days in captivity). Based on our aging research, lemon sharks grow very slowly and reach sexual maturity at 12 to 15 years of age and 8 to 10 feet in length. This pattern is typical of many other shark species. The oldest lemon shark we examined using vertebral ring counts was 31 years old. However, this does not imply that lemon sharks only live 31 years. Some species of sharks can live 75 to 100 years and maybe more. It is difficult to tell a shark's age based on its size, because sharks grow so slowly after they reach maturity. For instance, a shark that is 8 feet long may be 12 years old, but a shark that is 9 feet long may be 30 years old. That is why accurate age assessment determined by vertebral ring counts is so important in fisheries management.

As a result of their K-selected life history strategy, (see "Life Style of the Sharks" in this book) sharks grow slowly, mature late in life, produce few offspring, and live to be quite old — so they are prone to overharvesting. Sharks simply do not grow, mature, or replace themselves fast enough to maintain their population when typical fishing pressures are placed on them. This is in direct contrast to many other fish species with r-selected life history strategies characterized by fast growth, early maturity, many offspring, and a short life span. Obviously, before any type of fishery can be set up, much information is needed about the biology of shark species, especially the assessment of age. Blind management of a shark fishery will surely end in economic disaster for the fisherman and population disaster for the shark.

ADDITIONAL READING:

Budker, P. 1971. THE LIFE OF SHARKS. Columbia Univ. Press, New York.

Compagno, L.J.V. 1990. Shark exploitation and conservation. NOAA, NMFS Tech. Bull. (in press).

Cook, S. (ed). 1987. Sharks: An Inquiry into Biology, Behavior, Fisheries and Use. Oregon State Univ. Ext. Ser. Portland.

Moss, S. 1984. SHARKS. AN INTRODUCTION FOR THE AMATEUR NATURALIST. Prentice Hall. Englewood Cliffs, New Jersey.

Prince, E.D. and L.M. Pulos (ed.). 1983. Proceedings of the International Workshop on Age Determination of Oceanic Pelagic Fishes: Tunas, Billfishes, and Sharks. NOAA Tech. Rept. 8.

Springer, V.G. and J.P. Gold. 1989. SHARKS IN QUESTION. Smithsonian Inst. Press. Washington, DC.

U.S. Shark Fishery Management For The Atlantic Ocean

by THOMAS B. HOFF and JOSÉ I. CASTRO

Most sharks are predators at the top of the food chain, and so they in turn have few predators upon them. Juvenile sharks, because of their comparatively large size, have fewer predators than the minute juveniles of most bony fishes. Only the largest adult predatory sharks such as the white, mako, bull, and tiger can prey on smaller adult sharks. Thus, after 400 million years of evolution, sharks are adapted to having reduced predation as adults. Now, sharks face a new predator in the marine environment: man and his technology. Sharks are being harvested in such tremendous numbers that they may be unable to adapt to this new predator before their existence is threatened.

Although also harvested for their fins, skin, teeth, liver oil, and cartilage, most sharks in the world are caught for their meat. Annual landings are nearly 500,000 metric tons. Historically, directed shark fisheries have been small, short-lived, "boom and bust" enterprises where shark populations are rapidly reduced below sustainable levels. It is estimated that most shark species cannot withstand a fishing mortality as low as 5% per year (removal of 5% of the existent population each year) indefinitely.

Sharks are slow-growing, late-maturing fishes with gestation periods of up to two years. Many species pup in alternate years. This low reproductive potential is compensated for by young that hatch or are born fully developed and have low natural mortality. On the other hand, the

---

Hoff is a biologist/statistician with the Mid Atlantic Fishery Management Council, Dover, DE. Castro is a fishery biologist and shark specialist with NMFS Southeast Fisheries Center, Miami, FL.

evolutionary trade-off for fully developed young is that very few progeny can be produced at any one time.

U.S. Fisheries Management

The Magnuson Fishery Conservation and Management Act was passed in 1976 to manage and conserve the fishery resources of the United States. The Act established a 200-mile exclusive economic zone (EEZ) around the United States. Within the EEZ, the United States has exclusive fishery management authority over all fishery resources, except for tunas. Eight Regional Fishery Management Councils were set up to prepare plans for each fishery requiring conservation and management. The Councils submit their management plans to the Secretary of Commerce for implementation. To date 24 plans have been prepared for fisheries such as the American lobster, Atlantic billfishes, snapper-grouper, and Gulf of Mexico shrimp.

Work on a shark fisheries management plan was begun as a result of recreational and commercial shark fishing industries development in the late 1970's. However, due to insufficient fisheries and biological information, that plan was never completed. In the late 1980's spurred by the opening of shark fin markets in the Far East, the commercial shark fishing industry expanded rapidly. Since 1986, commercial shark landings have doubled every year. This rapid growth prompted the Councils to seek immediate shark fishery regulation. The known vulnerability of shark stocks to overfishing indicated that immediate action was needed to avoid a fishery collapse. The Councils agreed that a management plan could be developed more quickly if the Secretary of Commerce worked through

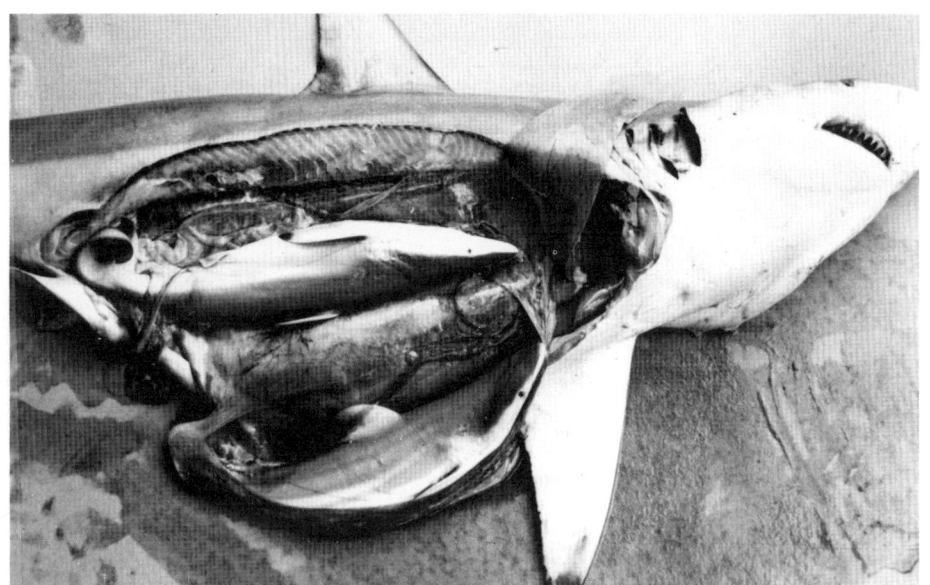
Blacktip shark bearing two pups. Most large coastal shark species bear from two to 12 young.

the National Marine Fisheries Service. In June 1989, the Councils asked the Secretary to develop and implement a plan to protect the east coast shark resources including United States waters of the Atlantic, Gulf of Mexico, and Caribbean.

Secretarial Plan

The Secretarial plan addresses the following problems: (1) overfishing, (2) lack of management, (3) increasing US landings, (4) "finning" or the practice of landing only fins and discarding the rest of the carcass, (5) bycatch mortality, (6) inadequate fisheries and biological information, (7) limited public education, and (8) habitat losses and degradation.

The plan objectives are: (1) to prevent overfishing, (2) to encourage management of shark stocks throughout their range, (3) to establish a data collection, research, and monitoring program, and (4) to optimize the benefit to the U.S. derived from shark resources while minimizing waste, consistent with the other objectives.

A fishery management plan must comply with the seven national standards of the Magnuson Act. The first is, "conservation and management measures shall prevent overfishing..." which the shark plan defines as a fishing mortality within U.S. waters that exceeds the estimated maximum sustainable yield estimate of 16,250 metric tons (slightly over 35 million pounds). Developed a decade ago, this estimate includes all mortality sources from the directed commercial, non-directed commercial, and recreational shark fisheries. Over the past decade, total mortality has exceeded the maximum yield estimate by nearly 6,000 metric tons annually. It is believed that the proposed management measures in addition to the mandatory use of turtle excluder devises (TEDs) in the shrimp fishery (which will also exclude sharks), and the proposed reduction of the swordfish fishery with its significant shark bycatch, will reduce shark mortality below the level of overfishing.

Management Measures

The proposed management measures are: (1) an annual quota for commercial landings of 5,800 metric tons, (2) a recreational bag limit of two sharks

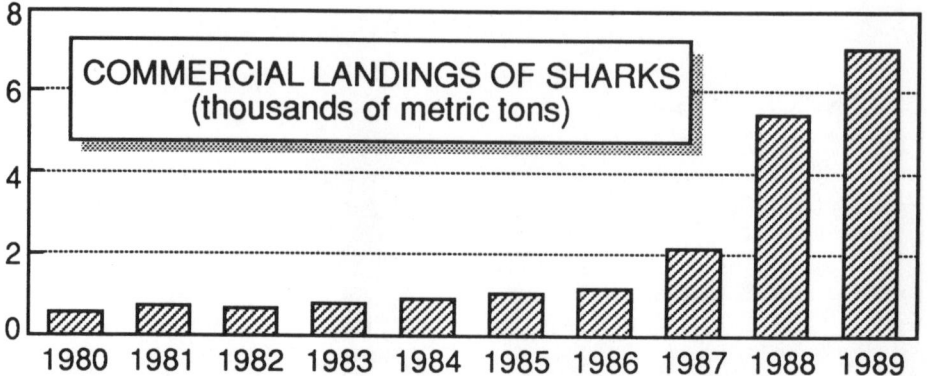

(other than sharpnose sharks), or four sharpnose sharks per angler per boat, (3) a procedure for annual adjustments in management measures, (4) prohibition of "finning," (5) prohibition of the sale of sharks caught by recreational fishermen, (6) annual permits for commercial fishermen and dealers, (7) a minimum size limit for mako sharks of 1.68 meters or about 5.5 feet long, and (8) data reporting for permitted fishermen, dealers, and tournament directors.

Public hearings held in December 1989, generated extensive interest and comments which are being used to improve the plan. Many individuals and organizations asked for even more stringent measures than those proposed. However, the urgency for management precludes more stringent measures and the ensuing debate would further delay implementation of the plan.

The annual adjustment procedure permits a quick response to the changing condition of the resources, and eliminates the need for time-consuming amendments to the plan.

The final management measures are not yet known, but probably will not differ greatly from the draft. The very existence of the resource is threatened as attempts are made to perfect a plan which resolves all the issues.

ADDITIONAL READING:

Castro, J.I. 1983. THE SHARKS OF NORTH AMERICAN WATERS. Texas A & M University Press. College Station, Texas. 180 p.

U. S. Department of Commerce. 1989. DRAFT SECRETARIAL SHARK FISHERY MANAGEMENT PLAN FOR THE ATLANTIC OCEAN, NMFS. St. Petersburg, Florida. 116 p.

Daily catch by one small-scale South Atlantic commercial shark fisherman.

The Only Good Shark Is a Dead Shark?

by SAMUEL H. GRUBER and CHARLES A. MANIRE

In the affairs of man, attitudes count and slogans reflecting those attitudes often lead to action. Consider "Just say no to drugs." First, there is a media blitz to raise public awareness. Then Columbian druglords are hunted down and extradited. The Panamanian dictator is toppled, and U.S. warships are on the move.

When it comes to relations with our fellow earthlings, the animals, human attitudes and slogans often spell the difference between survival and complete extinction. "Save the whales," "Protect the turtles," and "Cherish the rain forest" are, thankfully, refrains heard today with increasing clarity. Aggressive conservation groups such as Greenpeace backed by the more politically savvy Audubon Society and World Wildlife Fund, have raised public consciousness and nearly every educated American is aware that African rhino and elephant are being hunted to extinction.

But, when it comes to sharks (and their relatives), one of the most ancient, highly evolved, adapted, and diverse groups of animals on the planet, the prevailing Western attitude is *"the only good shark is a dead shark."* Unlike the whale, sea turtle, and sea otter, endearing animals that have been brought back from the brink of extinction, the shark has no broad constituency. Although the situation has improved since 1975 when the movie "Jaws" spawned a frenzy of fear and loathing of sharks, the people most concerned with sharks today are commercial, and to some extent recreational, fishermen who kill sharks — most often as quickly as possible. And there are essentially no limits or constraints on the killing.

This unrestrained slaughter is systematic, obscenely wasteful, and worldwide in scope. If this slaughter continues unabated, we believe that many shark stocks will be permanently damaged and marine environments thrown out of balance with unknown but certainly unhappy consequences. We submit that sharks are a key factor in the health and maintenance of marine food webs and that their demise must be avoided.

While sharks are not as "cute" as dolphins, they are also not the nightmare creatures of lore and in truth are amazing and wonderful animals with unjustly bad reputations. In this special issue of Underwater Naturalist we hope to influence attitudes so that knowledge of the important role of sharks may overshadow the prevailing irrational, centuries-old hatred.

In the Western mind the word shark conjures up a primitive, cold-blooded, man-eater, constantly roving the seas in search of and attacking human prey. The victim is torn to pieces and consumed by this diabolical creature from Hell. The truth is so different from the Jaws-like caricature that one wonders how it developed, and, in this age of information, how it survives. Part of the answer is that old attitudes are hard to dispel no matter what the facts.

The word, shark, is derived from the derogatory middle English word, *shurke* meaning villain. Today we talk of pool sharks and loan sharks. Outrageous and greedy corporate raiders are also called sharks as in the best seller SWIMMING WITH SHARKS.

But sharks are not motivated by greed or avarice, and they are certainly not

Gruber is professor of marine biology and fisheries at the University of Miami's Rosenstiel School of Marine and Atmospheric Science. He is director of the Bimini Biological Field Station, founder and a distinguished fellow of the American Elasmobranch Society, and has studied shark biology and behavior since 1961. Manire, a veterinarian, has worked with Gruber for the past three years.

Great hammerhead. Photo by J. Stafford-Deitsch.

man-killers. Of the 350 or so species, about 80% are unable to hurt people (too small, minute teeth, etc.) or never encounter people (living in the deep sea or Arctic waters).

Of those capable of hurting humans, only three or four species have the jaw structure and feeding ecology to consider human swimmers as legitimate prey.

The majority of shark attacks are motivated by social factors such as fear or "territoriality." The feeding drive apparently plays no role in over 50% of the recorded attacks. Most attacking sharks have the teeth, jaws, and strength to remove large portions from the fragile human body. Yet, an attack frequently consists of a single bite or bump perhaps resulting in serious laceration but no tissue removal. Are sharks trying to feed when they attack inedible steel boats, oceanographic instruments, or navigational buoys?

So, while sharks do attack people, such attacks are exceedingly rare and usually not lethal. In light of statistics automobiles, aircraft, elephants, bees, and man's best friend, the dog, should be hated and feared far more than the relatively innocuous shark. But when it comes to attitudes about sharks, the facts are usually irrelevant. There is something irrational and dark, way down in the subconscious that produces our unwarranted revulsion for sharks.

Surprisingly, not all societies consider sharks evil. Pacific Islanders who have a far more intimate relation with sharks and dependence on the ocean, do not fear sharks. Rather they respect and even revere them as the lords of the sea. In fact, sharks play a significant and positive role in the lore and mythology of Polynesia. So Western attitudes toward sharks cannot be innate or fixed. We should be able to reform them as we have done for other "man-eating" animals and base them on an enlightened understanding of the shark's true role and position on the evolutionary scale.

Yet another fairy tale reinforced by the Hollywood mythmakers is that sharks are primitive, prehistoric eating machines. From our studies we know that lemon sharks are on a strict feeding schedule dictated by their slow digestion rates. They ordinarily do not feed for 40-80 hours after taking a single meal that amounts to only 5% of their body weight on average. In the laboratory, they will ignore excess food once they are fed a meal equivalent to 2.7% of their body weight and cannot be induced to feed again for a day or so. Thus, unlike domestic dogs or humans, sharks simply will not overeat. So, sharks are definitely not "eating machines."

Are they primitive and prehistoric? If you lived in the Miocene, about 50 million years ago, you could catch fish like salmon, tarpon, or bonefish and easily recognize them as such. But try as you might you couldn't catch a hammerhead. They simply didn't exist yet. It would be another 5-10 million years before they came on the scene. In fact, much of the early evolution of the "advanced" teleost (bony) fishes was complete before the first cartilaginous fish appeared.

True, sharks have by-in-large retained the body shape and structure perfected millions of years ago and have been evolutionarily conservative. But this was after a period of intense and bizarre experimentation with body types some 300 million years ago. Eventually, the order that sharks belong to (elasmobranchs) settled on three basic groups: sharks, skates, and rays.

Are they primitive? The facts indicate otherwise. The 350 species of sharks present many "advanced" features such as internal fertilization, placental nourishment of the fetus, electroreception, social hierarchies, complicated kidneys, mobile eye pupils, magnetic navigation, and group feeding, to name just a few. Unfortunately, we do not yet know that much about shark biology to add to and complete this list. It is our sincere hope that sharks will be permitted to exist at least long enough to find out how they work.

After evolving and prospering for 400 million years or so, sharks and their allies are today faced with a survival crisis. In an evolutionary instant, man, the supreme predator, challenged them for dominance in the sea and predictably won. In 1989, more than 100,000,000 elasmobranchs were killed by the activities of man. That works out to about one million sharks killed for every person bitten, a heavy toll to pay. Of the estimated 4,000,000 sharks caught in the Western North Atlantic about 80% were killed and dumped back into the sea. It is difficult to think of a more appropriate example of "senseless slaughter,"— wasteful in the extreme. The high seas longline fisheries that specialize in pelagic fishes such as tuna and billfish are perhaps the worst perpetrators. This non-selective fishing method produces a huge shark by-catch that is simply worth too little to take up space in the ship's hold. Result: millions of dead sharks, rotting on the bottom.

As if this were not enough, a new wasteful market has arisen — finning. Coming on the heels of Asian prosperity, the world-wide demand for shark fins to produce esoteric Oriental dishes has skyrocketed. In Florida alone, landings have doubled annually for the past three years with an estimated 100,000 sharks taken in 1989 exclusively for the Asian fin market. What happens is this: the shark is captured, usually in a gill net, three of the eight fins cut off and the dead or dying shark discarded. This means that 98% of the useful protein is wasted. And, horribly, some of the sharks recover from the butchery only to slowly starve to death. The rest decay on the seabed. When the Miami Herald broke this story in 1989, there was widespread revulsion and for the first time, attitudes toward sharks began to shift a bit.

The worst offender, in terms of pure

Blue sharks caught in a shark fishing tournament. Photo by S. Gruber.

unselective slaughter, is the floating gill net industry. High tech, mechanized fleets deploy nets more than 30 miles long. When these synthetic fiber nets are inadvertently lost, they passively move through the seas, essentially forever, like a plague, trapping and killing every large creature in their wake. Again, economics take precedence, and sharks and other low value fishes and marine mammals are discarded. Happily, use of these floating death nets is being outlawed on an international basis, but they are still out there.

The common response to all of this is still, so what? Isn't there an endless supply of sharks like other fishes? Even if not, wouldn't we be better off by getting rid of all the sharks anyway? The answer is an emphatic no.

Fossil records from 350 million years ago demonstrate that the cartilaginous fishes had settled upon a life history strategy very different from their bony cousins. Clear evidence of claspers and sex organs signaling internal fertilization, combined with fossils of pregnant shark-like fishes show that heavy parental investment in a few, well developed offspring was the rule for sharks then as now. The implication of this life history pattern which ecologists call K-selected after the mathematical symbol "K" for the capacity of an ecosystem to "carry" or support a species, is that the number of young is severely limited by the very low fecundity of the parents. In such a system, the parents usually grow slowly, mature late in life, and live for a long time.

The K-selected life history pattern is an evolutionary winner under conditions of environmental stability. Sharks and other K-selected creatures such as sea turtles and whales bet their existence on a stable food supply, continuously available living space, and a balanced, stable death rate that does not fluctuate much from year to year to year. Disturb these conditions and the odds become stacked against them. Eventually they lose the bet. The inevitable result is population crash and even extinction.

Bony fishes evolved a very different life style characterized by rapid growth, short life span, and external fertilization combined with incredibly high fecundity. Some fish mothers produce hundreds of thousands of eggs each season, but the babies are very fragile and infant mortality is extremely high. Ecologists call this pattern r-selected and believe its chief adaptation is to a relatively unstable, fluctuating environment. Bony fishes are considered the pioneers of the marine world, ready by virtue of their high fecundity to take advantage of any new supportive habitat. They can also weather natural disasters such as unexpected temperature fluctuations when models based on teleost (bony fish) life histories cannot work for sharks.

These concepts are not merely theoretical constructs. The history of shark fisheries has been characterized by a consistent boom and bust pattern. In this case, bust means that the population of sharks has been so rapidly and completely decimated that fishermen cannot capture enough to make it worthwhile, bad for the fisherman but even worse for the shark.

Costly shark products. Photo by S. Gruber.

most of the adults are killed. This is because a few, very fertile mothers can quickly reconstitute the population, an adaptation impossible for today's sharks.

The practical result of the r- and K-selected strategies is that fishery managers often talk of the relation between stock and recruitment. They say that for fishes, stock is unrelated to recruitment while for sharks, stock and recruitment are directly related. For fishes, recruitment, the growing up of young into the general population, depends more on favorable conditions for the survival of babies than the number of mothers in the population. In contrast, the new members of a shark population are directly dependent on numbers of reproductively active shark mothers. Thus, unlike fishes, the supply of sharks is extremely limited and that's why fishery

The porbeagle (mackerel) shark fishery of the Western North Atlantic is one of the best documented. This sleek, swift, pelagic predator was swept from North Atlantic waters in only seven years. In the late 1950's, Italians considered porbeagle flesh a gourmet delight and were willing to pay exorbitant prices for it. Norwegian fishermen, familiar with the species' habits were more than happy to reap this windfall. In 1961, the uncontrolled exploitation began and about 3,500,000 pounds were caught. The catch quickly peaked only three years later at 16 million pounds, then crashed. By 1968 only a few hundred sharks could be found. Now, over 20 years later, populations have not returned to pre-exploitation levels. Virtually the same story can be told for the Californian thresher and soupfin shark fisheries, the Irish basking shark fishery, the Lake Nicaraguan bull shark fishery, the Virginian sandbar shark fishery, and so on. This irrational exploitation must be controlled not only because of the intrinsic value of the sharks, but because of their important role in maintaining an ecological balance in the seas.

How can sharks possibly be of any benefit to the marine environment or to man? Most sharks occupy the position of apex predator in their environment. This means that they occupy the top of the food web with few or no natural enemies. Like all apex predators, the sharks benefit organisms below them in the food web in several ways and thereby also indirectly benefit humans. By killing less fit members the shark clearly benefits other individuals of that species as well as future generations.

Predators generally feed on individuals easy to capture, such as the weak, very old, or young. By feeding on sick individuals, sharks help keep disease under control. Massive epidemics become rare events, thus keeping the prey species healthy. By feeding on the weak, sharks allow more fit individuals to survive and reproduce. Reproduction by such strong individuals is likely to produce stronger offspring which also benefits the species. By feeding on the old and feeble, sharks remove these individuals from competition for limited space, food, or other resources, thereby providing more survival time for younger, more reproductively active individuals. Finally, by feeding on the very young the weaker, slower, less fit young are removed from the population before having an opportunity to reproduce. Again, this leads to more fit adults which in turn produce more fit offspring. The Darwinian benefits to the species as a whole become clear. The indirect benefits to humans come in the form of a more stable, healthier food supply derived from the oceans. Although some fishermen view sharks as competitors for the same fish, sharks generally tend to take the individuals which might be culled anyway by the fishermen. By stretching the point, one could say that sharks insure the fisherman of a good supply from which to select.

These potential benefits to prey species are widespread. The 350 species of sharks, all predators, are distributed in virtually all marine habitats and even some fresh-water rivers and lakes about the world. They continuously exert selection pressure through predation and thereby benefit thousands of prey species. An additional benefit is that diversity is maintained in the oceans by preventing explosions of single species which might dominate specific food supplies causing other species to die out.

While some of the beneficial evolutionary controls exerted by sharks as apex predators are rather speculative (i.e., not "proven" according to strict scientific guidelines) one can easily see that there is a definite place in the scheme of things for sharks. So, from a biological viewpoint, the best shark is one which is alive and well and doing what comes naturally. Thus it is time for the negative attitude toward sharks to be replaced with a realistic view, so that the senseless slaughter will be replaced by rational use and conservation of an invaluable group of animals.

Note: If our plea has moved you to action, write to the appropriate state official and legislators about your concern for this wanton, uncontrolled, and ecologically destructive slaughter. The Federal Government has moved decisively to protect sharks in federal waters, i.e., beyond the three mile limit. If implemented, the National Marine Fisheries Service plan will stop the slaughter, but only about 20% of shark fishing occurs beyond the three-mile limit. This means that the lion's share of sharks are caught in state waters which are not bound by any federal management plans. Should the federal "Secretarial Shark Management Plan" be implemented, it could become a model for state legislation. If the coastal states adopt the plan, we are certain localized shark stocks will recover. However, the majority of commercial species undertake long migrations, often crossing national boundaries. So the ultimate goal of any conservation plan should be the adoption of a multinational program of "shark consciousness." Your help could be decisive.

ADDITIONAL READING:

Gruber, S.H. and C.A. Manire, 1989. Challenge of the Chondrichthyans. Chondros 1(1):1-3.

Gruber, S.H. and C.A. Manire, 1990. A finful of dollars. BBC Wildlife 8(4):234-239.

Gruber, S.H. and J.F. Morrissey, 1990. Shark vs. man: Are sharks losing the battle? Underwater Naturalist 19(1):3-7.

Manire, C.A. and S.H. Gruber, 1990. Many sharks may be headed toward extinction. Conservation Biology 4(1):10-11.

Tiger shark caught alive without fins. Photo by G. Myers.

The Sharks' Side. . .

Products that prey on shark wimps

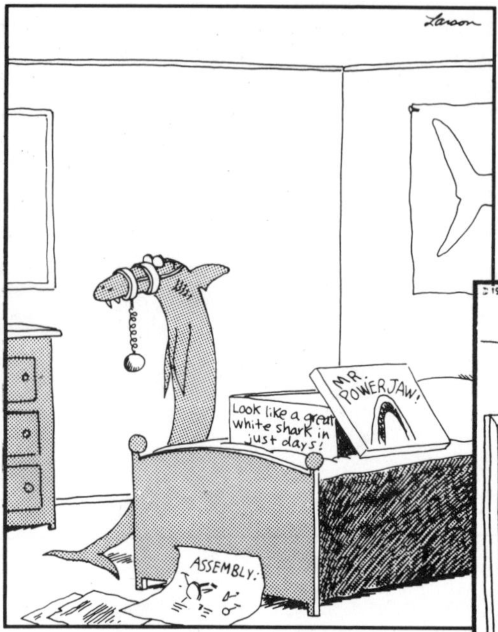

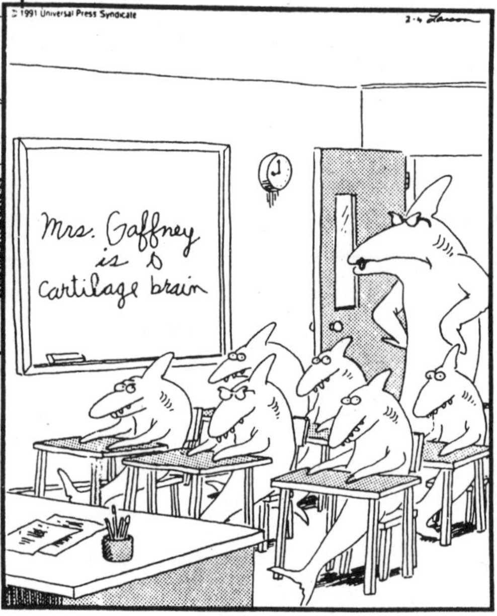

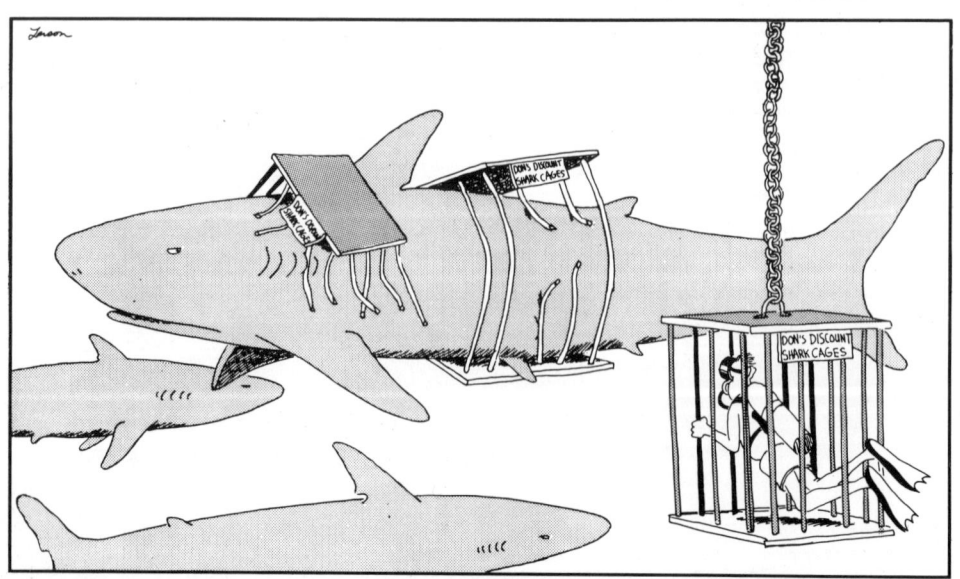